P9-DVT-351

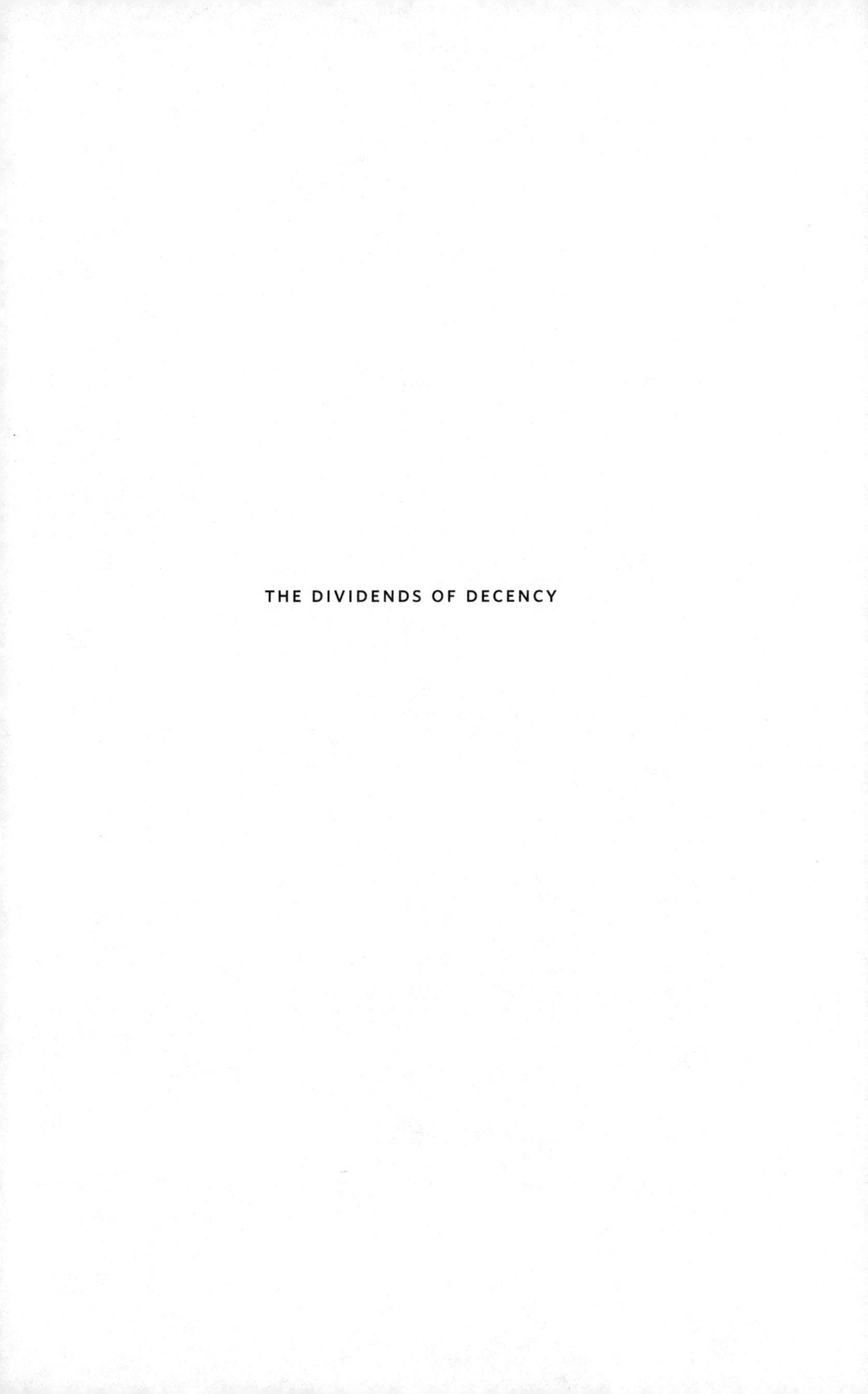

THE DIVIDENDS OF DECENCY

How Values-Based Leadership Will Help Business Flourish in Trump's America

DONALD
LEE SHEPPARD

with John Lawrence Reynolds

The Dividends of Decency

Figure.1

Vancouver / Berkeley

18 19 20 21 22 5 4 3 2 1

Cataloguing data is available from Library and Archives Canada
ISBN 978-1-77327-032-6 (hbk.)
ISBN 978-1-77327-033-3 (ebook)
ISBN 978-1-77327-034-0 (pdf)

Cover design by Milène Vallin and Jessica Sullivan
Interior design by Naomi MacDougall
Author photograph by Steven Nilsson Photography
Editing by Karen Milner
Copy editing by Lindsay Humphreys
Proofreading by Renate Preuss
Indexing by Stephen Ullstrom

Printed and bound in Canada by Friesens
Distributed in the United States by
Publishers Group West

Figure 1 Publishing Inc.
Vancouver BC Canada
www.figure1publishing.com

For my wife and partner, Cayce Brooks Malone, who never wavered in her support for me and whose strength, power and brilliance serve as the tail to my kite.

For our children, Morgan Jane and Donald Malone Sheppard, who exemplify all the good qualities I celebrate in this book and whose achievements make my heart swell with love and pride.

And for the over-achieving honorable team at Sheppard Associates, who proved the power of values-based leadership—I wish we were still together.

Contents

PROLOGUE xi

PART ONE

Character Counts

1 The Company That Lost Its Balance 3

2 Business Ethics: An Oxymoron That Needn't Be 15

3 Measures of Integrity 29

4 How the Pursuit of Profit Can Make You Blind—and Maybe Deaf as Well 47

5 Das Auto. Die Dummkopfs. 63

6 Did We Not Get the Enron Memo? 71

7 Deeds, Not Words (1) 79

PART TWO

From Tar-Paper Shack to Paneled Boardroom

8 How Do You Know When You're Wealthy? 91

9 When They Need You More than You Need Them 109

10 A New Way of Looking at Work 123

11 Deeds, Not Words (2) 137

12 "How're You Doin' Now, Sucker?" 145

PART THREE

Take It from the Top: The Fundamental Role of Values-Based Leadership

13 Who Matters Most? 155

14 Integrity: The Difference between Leaders and Rulers 163

15 Ethics: Define Them, Live Them 169

16 Diversity: The Secret Ingredient of Successful Companies 179

17 Values and the Future of American Business 185

18 Why Trust Matters 193

A FURIOUS FINAL WORD 203

ACKNOWLEDGEMENTS 205

ENDNOTES 207

INDEX 211

“We are not studying in order to know what virtue is, but to become good, for otherwise there would be no profit in it.”

ARISTOTLE, 320 BC

“Ethics is what you do when no one is looking.”

GEORGE BERNARD SHAW

Prologue

YES, ANOTHER BOOK decrying the fact that the United States of America, the bastion of freedom and justice, chose Donald J. Trump as its president.

But this book is different.

There are many reasons to go on record denouncing Trump's various failings and how they are in direct conflict with this country's values and traditions. I'm dealing here with the one that risks making a deep and indelible impact on the manner in which business is conducted in the United States: his ethics. (Correction: his lack of ethics.)

Trump's misogynist attitudes, tolerance of racist and extreme right-wing groups, narrow vision, autocratic style and general demeanor have outraged me as much as any other American, not to mention the rest of the world. This is in addition to his ignorance of the way the U.S. federal government functions, his insulting attitudes to various American allies and economic partners, and his general incompetence at achieving anything except eliminating the achievements of his predecessors. Sheesh.

Trump has also made it clear, from his words and his actions, that he has a complete disregard for doing business in a principled way. His many millions of dollars have been made, several times over, at the expense of others and of the system—the written and unwritten rules of business. The worst part is not that he has been successful despite his bluster and disdain for business ethics (although that's bad enough) but that his public endorsement of success at any cost—and now his endorsement of this from a position of incredible power—will rub off on others and lower the bar generally on how business is done in this country. The risk of this—in both the short term and the long term—cannot be underestimated and could represent one of the darkest corners of Trump's legacy.

To whatever extent Donald Trump extends his influence, his unprincipled actions threaten to lower the level of ethics and values in America below its already diminished point. Nothing in the man's background suggests that his standards approach the level we have a right to expect from our leaders. Americans, like every society down through history, are influenced by the values and deeds of their leaders. Good and bad actions of leaders are absorbed and emulated by those whom they govern. Citizens of democracies such as the United States are as vulnerable to this form of influence as any society, and I worry that because Trump is a businessperson first and foremost, his negative influence may affect corporate America in particular. Are we at risk of our future business leaders thinking that Trump is the paragon of power and entrepreneurial success? Will they justify shady or unethical behavior on the basis that, if our president can ignore basic principles to reach the top, anything goes for anyone? Do we really want our corporate leaders of tomorrow to believe that the end justifies the means?

The prospect frightens me, just as much as it should frighten other Americans who value what this country stands for. American business is the engine of our economy and a key driver of our country's power and influence on the world stage. Nothing could damage that position more than a decline in our corporate standards of decency, honesty and integrity. We've seen it happen with the financial crisis of

2008 and with other corporate scandals, but it is my belief that with Donald Trump in the White House, the decline in ethics will be even more precipitous, making a negative impact on our country's future generally and rubbing off on corporate America specifically.

I am here to tell you that there is a better way—a more principled path to leading a company and a country. I'm speaking as a businessperson who achieved success without resorting to or even contemplating some of the tactics that Donald Trump has employed over his career. I believe that the vast majority of successful and dedicated businesspeople feel as I do: if you can't make it in business by maintaining a reasonable degree of ethics, find something else to do. Those of us who built and operate businesses that treat employees fairly, and contribute to the wealth of communities generally, need not only to disagree publicly with Trump's way of doing business but also to take action to mitigate the impact his influence can have on this country.

All of this may be a revelation to the large numbers of Americans who sincerely believed that America would benefit by having an experienced businessperson in the White House. Successful CEOs, they proposed, know how to manage complex organizations by improving efficiency, slashing waste, controlling spending and demonstrating good leadership qualities. It all sounds convincing on paper, but reality has a way of shredding paper-based expectations.

America is not a corporation. It is a democracy that honors and values diverse viewpoints and obligations. Unlike competitive businesses, its success is measured neither by quarterly profit reports, stock market share price nor competitive position. Moreover, many of its most important strategic decisions are made not within the confines of a boardroom and then communicated via confidential memos; they are made in open debate and discussion, subject to approval or rejection in a supposedly free ballot. And while open criticism of a corporate CEO by an employee of the firm may lead to serious consequences, citizens of a free democracy are not only permitted to challenge their leaders' decisions, they are encouraged to do so through their involvement in the democratic process. Add the reality of partisan politics and bureaucratic structure and other distractions, and the transition between CEO and democratic leaders does not look seamless—it looks virtually impossible.

In November 2016, the advocates of "Let's put a businessperson in the White House!" got their wish. In return, America and the rest of the world got a basket of headaches, farce, embarrassment, dismissals, chaos and serious questions about illegal influence on the democratic process that represents the very essence of the country's longtime and hard-earned status, power and position on the world stage. Anyone who believes that Donald Trump has validity as either an astute businessperson or a world leader should review the experience of his much-vaunted Manufacturing Councils.

Within weeks of his election—and well before his inauguration—Trump announced that he would be chairing two councils: "... some of America's most highly respected and successful business leaders will be called upon to meet with the President frequently to share their specific experience and knowledge as the President implements his economic agenda."[1] They were an impressive group, including Elon Musk of Tesla; Stephen Schwarzman, CEO of Blackstone; Jack Welch, former CEO of GE; and top executives from some of the biggest, most respected companies in the United States—PepsiCo, Disney, General Motors, Boeing and others.

It's fair to say that a no-more-extraordinary assembly of business minds had ever before come together for the purpose of advising a new president in America's history. Certainly, none had ever collapsed as quickly. Within six months, two key members, Musk and Robert Iger of Disney, resigned in protest of Trump's decision to withdraw from the Paris Agreement on climate change. Two months later, so many others jumped ship that Trump dissolved both groups to save face. With his words and manner, especially with regard to racist problems such as those that occurred in Charlottesville, Virginia, in the summer of 2017, Trump made it increasingly difficult for his chosen "advisers" to fall back on the "business is business" justification for continuing to deal with him.

Just how effective is a businessperson as a political leader when the top businesspeople in the country cannot work with him?

Donald Trump's ignorance of the chasm between business and politics has never been more vividly illustrated—and, in my view, inherently dangerous—than his belief that he can demand personal loyalty from members of his cabinet and those in key positions such as the director of the FBI. The first loyalty of every federal government official is and must always be to the United States of America; to the principles and standards upheld in the Constitution and in the office of the presidency. This loyalty should not be, and was never intended to be, sworn to any individual in any position, including the president. Of all the crevasses separating the two roles of corporate CEO and U.S. president, none is wider, deeper and more treacherous to cross than this one. CEOs can expect or even demand loyalty from their staff; U.S. presidents have no right to do the same thing, a fact that Trump either does not know or refuses to acknowledge. I suspect he knows and simply doesn't care, which is another measure of the man's ethics.

On their own, Donald Trump's business practices reflect badly on American society generally. His ability to gather such wealth and power while rejecting so many of the values that Americans have held dear—and that much of the world has long admired and often emulated—is surely an indictment of sorts on our penchant for rewarding image over values. Trump's insistence on applying these stained values as the basis for his qualifications as POTUS sets the country on a downward spiral, a vicious circle of ever-diminishing principles.

The impact of Trump's warped sense of values extends beyond news items and the efforts of stand-up comedians striving to stay ahead of his outrageous antics. He is at the helm of the world's greatest democracy, a country that has stood as the bastion of freedom and justice for almost two and a half centuries. The rest of the world either smiles or shudders at his latest escapade or scandal and thinks, *Is this how American businesspeople act? Are these the values of American business and the country's society in general?*

Trump's influence in our own backyard may be even more devastating and enduring. All leaders are models, and the more visible and powerful the model, the deeper and wider the impact made. If the president of the United States has had to defend himself in almost two thousand court cases linked to his business dealings,[2] has declared corporate bankruptcy at least four times,[3] has been named in allegations of sexual assault or harassment a number of times and refuses to divest himself of his investments while in office to eliminate the possibility of collusion, why should the CEO in Chicago or the hardware dealer in San Jose or the salesman in Atlanta behave differently?

LET'S GET ANY prejudices on the record and out of the way from the start.

I am one of 66 million U.S. citizens who voted against Donald Trump becoming president—which, if you care to deal in numbers, was about 3 million more than voted for him. You could add to this the 80 million or so voters who stayed home on November 8, 2016, many of whom were convinced that Trump couldn't possibly win. But he did, and none of our grumbling or speculating can change this fact.

In some nations, the matter would end there. If you or I lived in one of those countries, we who awoke on November 9, 2016, asking ourselves, "What just happened?" would be ordered to accept the results and shut up about it. But we don't live in that kind of country (not yet anyway, I am inclined to add). In the United States, we're not ordered to shut up about anything our governments do if we seriously disagree with what they've done. We are expected—some would say obligated—to shout, stamp our feet and otherwise voice our complaints when an event occurs that risks damaging the freedom, opportunities and style of life that we cherish.

Donald Trump has made his influence on this country felt in various ways, and I am at a loss to identify any positive aspects. Many of his actions and attitudes, even just a few weeks into his occupation of the White House, trouble me. If you chose not to vote for Trump, I suspect that you and I find the same qualities of his disturbing. There are enough to fill not just this book but an entire library. This is not a man, let's remember, who simply occupies a seat in Congress or harangues us on Fox News. This is the individual (or at least the office) we tell our children to respect, admire and, I shudder to write, emulate. He is a leader, and among other duties, setting an ethical standard for the nation to follow is a leader's role.

We look to leaders for many things, among the most important of which are the values that leaders demonstrate in their behavior, both personal and official. It is impossible for anyone in a democracy to offer full support to a leader whose ethical standards conflict with his or her own. Nor, unfortunately, can some avoid being negatively influenced by a leader whose principles are questionable or hard to find at all.

Business ethics in America have hardly been pristine over the republic's years. We didn't need Donald Trump's presence in the White House to prompt the misdeeds of Bernie Madoff, Lehman Brothers and dozens of others. They managed to break or discard widely accepted organizational rules of behavior on their own. But their actions made clear the narrow band that exists between companies behaving as they should in a democratic free-enterprise system and those practicing whatever they can get away with in the pursuit of greater profit and wider power.

I speak from no remote ivory tower on the matter of business ethics. I achieved business success without academic credentials, social status or family connections but instead with dedication, hard work and applying high ethical standards in every transaction and at every level. This may make me admirable in the minds of some, but it does not make me heroic. I reject the idea that anyone can be lauded as a hero just for being honest, courteous and respectful.

I am deeply concerned, however, about a society that laughs off the behavior of its leader; behavior that would generate derision, rejection and prosecution if practiced by an ordinary citizen. This book reflects my concern, but my intention goes beyond simply voicing that. I am reaching out to other businesspeople and to Americans generally, urging them to view Trump not just as someone who insults various valued traditions of America but to see him also as a threat to America's trust and reliance on its business sector.

Here is my premise in three parts:

First, I'll delve deeply into the murky waters of low ethics as practiced not only by Trump himself but also by organizations and their leaders who found themselves caught up in the same kind of whirlpool surrounding Trump and his policies.

My effort to place my own professional life in context comes next. I cannot criticize anyone, even Trump, with such vehemence without presenting an example of how success in business can be achieved while maintaining one's own ethical standards. With that in mind, Part Two opens with the story of my early years growing up in an unheated home with no indoor plumbing amid a landscape that resembled the surface of the moon more than the one surrounding my current home in Southern California. The story I share recounts not only how I overcame these childhood challenges but also how they helped shape my values and ambition. I avoided stooping to behavior that would never be tolerated in a schoolyard or on a baseball diamond. It wasn't difficult for me and shouldn't be difficult for anyone, although it appears to be a challenge for the president of the United States of America.

Finally, the benefits of maintaining a standard of ethics, measured in multiple ways at various levels, are made clear in Part Three. As stunning as it may seem to those who accept Donald Trump's actions and values as appropriate business practice, there is more to be gained in the long run by behaving decently than there is to be gained from assuming the business world is some Wild West fantasy. The dividends of ethical business practices may not appear as dramatic as the pursuit of profit above all else, but they are far more sustainable and far less risky. They include attracting top-ranked employees, building both employee support and customer loyalty, avoiding legal costs and penalties, and generating healthier long-term profits. How's that for a multifaceted incentive?

Decency in business encompasses more than keeping your word in every transaction. It involves recognizing and responding to the needs and expectations of every group affected by a business organization—employees, customers, suppliers, partners, communities, markets and societies at large. We need to acknowledge this reality. More than that, we need to practice it in ways I'm about to explain. So pour yourself a coffee, sit back and kick off your shoes.

Speaking of shoes...

PART ONE

Character Counts

1

The Company That Lost Its Balance

AMONG ALL THE responses to the election of Donald Trump as President of the United States of America, at least one story didn't amount to much. Most Americans forgot about it as other events pushed it out of the picture. But the story symbolized something that could not be ignored.

It involved New Balance Athletics Inc., the Boston-based company best known for its sporting footwear. New Balance, despite its name, is hardly a new company. Founded in 1906, its annual sales volume has hovered around $4 billion for several years. Against competition from Nike, Adidas, Puma and other brands, it faces an uphill challenge, partly because it is among the last shoe companies to manufacture at least part of its product line in the United States. All of its major competitors make their shoes in China, Vietnam, Malaysia and elsewhere. The lower wages and other cost savings associated with doing business in those nations enable New Balance's competitors to undercut it in price.

New Balance insists on partially assembling some of its line of shoes in the United States, where it pays decent wages and is taxed at state and federal levels. The company recovers at least part of its higher costs by using its domestic manufacturing policy as a marketing tool. The company's pitch has been that you may pay a little more to purchase New Balance shoes, but you support American workers and American industry in the bargain. It's a plausible message, and along with other features—New Balance offers a choice of shoe widths that is much wider than its competitors, for example—it has served the firm well over the years.

Like many aspects of global business, it's easy to simplify things to support a chosen point of view. New Balance capitalizes on its domestic production, but not all its shoes are made in America. Most of its volume, by far, arrives from Vietnam, and the company maintains a factory in the United Kingdom to produce shoes for sale in its European markets. Nor is New Balance a major manufacturer of athletic wear generally. The number of the company's employees in the United States is dwarfed by the almost seven thousand factory workers in Nike's American plants (although most are admittedly busy producing athletic apparel other than shoes). Still, the firm has found a brand position, and positioning is critical in helping any company to cut through marketing and promotion clamor.

New Balance enjoys marketing leverage based on its plants in New England, and the company sought to make the most of it. So when Donald Trump shook not just the United States but also the rest of the world by being declared the winner of the 2016 presidential election, the company's VP of public affairs celebrated the event by declaring that the firm was looking forward to Trump assuming the office of the presidency.[4]

Why? Because Trump opposed the proposed Trans-Pacific Partnership (TPP), which would have cut import duties on products originating in much of Asia. The shoe firm's opinion had nothing to do with other qualities of Trump and his campaign promises. The spokesperson made no reference to Donald Trump's confessions about his misogynistic behavior, his multiple bankruptcies, his attitude toward minorities and people with disabilities or a dozen other unpleasant aspects of the man's values and behavior. The comment was only an observation on one specific aspect of Trump's policies and made by a spokesperson whose concern may have been legitimate but whose logic was essentially shabby. Anyone with knowledge of international business in the twenty-first century knows that capital is far easier to migrate than labor. The reasons behind the shift of manufacturing to countries beyond North America and Europe are complex, and their impact is permanent.*

Still, the idea that America has lost jobs to foreigners played well during the 2016 presidential election campaign. So well, in fact, that Trump's Democratic opponents Hillary Clinton and Bernie Sanders decried the TPP along with Trump. On that basis, the New Balance spokesperson might well have celebrated the election of either nominee had he or she defeated Trump. Had Clinton won, and had New Balance praised her policy, it probably wouldn't have generated a blip on the surface of the post-election news waves. But when the company spokesman praised Trump, the reaction was swift and intense.

Guilt by Association

When the *Wall Street Journal* ran the story about New Balance's satisfaction with Trump's victory, it unleashed storms from two opposing directions. From the right wing of American politics came rejoicing over New Balance's comment. The racist neo-Nazi blog *The Daily Stormer* declared New Balance "the official shoes of white people." Others on the extreme right celebrated in similar style.

The most powerful reaction, however, rose among Americans who didn't necessarily identify with either political wing. Their response to Trump's election and New Balance's half-hearted endorsement

* No one in industry seriously believes that the manufacturing jobs lost from the U.S. over the past three decades are going to return to America—especially old-school work like making sneakers. Many of those jobs were lost not just to foreign competition but also to automation. For example: The U.S. produces almost as much steel today as it did in 1990 but with one-tenth the number of workers. Robotic tools do most of the work that people once performed, and they do it accurately and safely twenty-four hours per day without striking for higher wages. They, not illegal immigrants or foreign workers, took jobs from middle-class Americans. TPP wouldn't threaten existing manufacturing jobs as much as they would encourage the U.S. to build sales volume from the export of IT services and programs.

was not just immediate but emphatically negative. Thousands of Americans made a point of publicly burning their New Balance shoes, raising such an outcry that it forced the shoe company to respond. In a statement issued three days later among other sources, the firm declared:

> New Balance does not tolerate bigotry or hate in any form. One of our officials was recently asked to comment on a trade policy that was taken out of context. As a 110-year-old company with five factories in the U.S. and thousands of employees worldwide from all races, genders, cultures and sexual orientations, New Balance is a values-driven organization and culture that believes in humanity, integrity, community and mutual respect for people around the world.

It served as a means of separating New Balance from the president-elect and setting the record straight, but the association with Trump continued to reverberate, shaking New Balance sales in dramatic fashion. One credible sales industry source claimed that within weeks of the statement praising Trump, sales of New Balance products dropped 23 percent in California, 17 percent in Oregon and a whopping 25 percent in New York State.[5] How much of those sales recovered when the memory of the New Balance spokesperson's slipup faded? It remains to be seen. The lesson to be learned, however, is clear.

Political pundits and philosophers are certain to argue for years to come over the consequences of Donald Trump's stunning victory in the 2016 presidential race. I have neither the insight nor the intent to deal with that aspect. I'm interested in the fact that an enormous number of Americans recoil from businesspeople whose actions and statements are (or appear to be) aligned with Trump's views and who are, therefore, in opposition to this country's fundamental ethical standards and values. This is what cost New Balance its abrupt drop in sales. And it is a lesson to American businesses generally about the value of operating with principles, fairness and equity, despite the immediate appeal of dispensing with those qualities in search of profit and sales status.

The lesson appears destined to be relearned and retaught over and over again. Like all lessons based on experience, the cost can be both painful and unnecessary.* What's more, the price is not immediately apparent, which makes it all the more tempting to discard ethics if the focus is fixed exclusively on the bottom line.

To be clear: The dividends earned from operating a business based on fairness to all concerned—employees, customers, suppliers and shareholders—are measured not only in potentially enhanced profits but in avoided costs as well. The most obvious example of the cost of unprincipled business practices is the loss of reputation suffered by companies whose management policies are revealed to be unfair, illegal or simply disrespectful to the wide communities they serve. Profits may be immediate, and vengeance can take time to arrive; when it does arrive, however, the damage it inflicts is both deep and widespread.

Risking Millions to Tell the Truth

The corporate fallout from Trump's victory didn't stop with the New Balance fiasco. Within a month of Trump's inauguration, another athletic company, Under Armour, found itself in similar straits after its CEO, Kevin Plank, praised the new president as "a real asset to this country." (NBA star Stephen Curry, who was receiving $4 million annually from Under Armour to endorse basketball shoes, quipped that he would agree with the assessment if Plank dropped the "et" from asset.)

This time the negative rebound arrived first from athletes and artists representing minorities in America. They included Misty Copeland, the first African-American principal dancer of the American Ballet Theatre, who declared that she had always spoken openly about the need for diversity and inclusion, adding, "It is imperative to me that my partners and sponsors share this belief."[6] Others added

* Learning through experience alone is not always practical and is rarely enjoyable. Marshall McLuhan once characterized experience as a source of wisdom by describing a condemned man being led to his execution and saying to himself, "This will teach me a lesson."

their voices to the dispute. Notable among them were investment industry analysts, at least one of whom dropped the target price for Under Armour stock from $40 to $24, or 40 percent.

Let's get it straight: I am not proposing that business leaders or any other group of Americans should muzzle their opinion of the country's leaders, all the way to the president. Our right to praise or criticize them must remain a pillar of our freedom. The CEOs of New Balance, Under Armour and every other organization must feel free to state their opinions if they so choose, and be prepared to accept the reaction they generate.

The New Balance and Under Armour incidents are notable because they confirmed a deep and abiding dislike of Trump among many Americans. The message here is that the pushback from the public was based more on Trump's lack of principles in general—his animosity to minority groups, his sneering attitude toward women, his bluster and insults, and his overall ethics (or lack of them)—rather than on his specific partisan politics.

The United States has had its share of often-violent responses to political events at the federal level. I remember clearly the hostility at the 1968 Democratic National Convention and the widespread revulsion that led to the resignation of President Richard Nixon six years later. These things occur when passion and politics mingle. They are a regretful by-product of our electoral process, but those of us committed to supporting a free society prefer them to the silence and fear imposed by a dictatorial regime intent on suppressing freedom.

Those who burned their shoes in protest of the presumed connection between Trump and New Balance may have overreacted, but the message was clear: Americans expect ethical conduct from their leaders. They have more than a right to demand this action; they have a duty to do so. When leaders demonstrate contempt for ethics, those who choose—or appear to choose—to support them become linked to them by association, and the public will respond accordingly.

The presidency of Donald Trump, elected despite his blemished record of personal and business behavior, has generated a ripple effect that may taint the reputation of American business. His identity as a businessperson represents the primary risk. Those in business who believe anything goes in pursuit of maximizing short-term profits may find solace in his example (assuming they are prepared to deal with near-incessant lawsuits and multiple bankruptcies). Americans who already view business with a jaundiced eye could believe their suspicions were confirmed by the arrival of this particular CEO in the White House. And nations beyond America, who represent both our export market potential and our key suppliers, may suspect that Trump's actions are both condoned and copied widely throughout the country, influencing their approach to trade with us, or at least their perception of how America does business.

A segment of American society obviously chose to disregard Trump's unsavory activities. Some defended them as exaggeration. Others rationalized them as campaign rhetoric or unfair criticism by his opponents. And still others, fundamentally aligned with Trump's views, equated his racist or sexist comments with their own. Whatever category they fell into, their support confirmed that portions of American society have long tolerated unethical practices by their politicians, business leaders and corporations. When this type of behavior generated widespread damage to some segments of the economy and no one was held accountable for it, many Americans were resigned to shrugging their shoulders. If Congress and the courts refused to grow troubled over such behavior, why—and how—should ordinary citizens react?*

Leaders tend to emulate the values and actions of other leaders—especially if those values and actions are associated with success. Trump's boorish behavior and lack of ethics did not preclude him from occupying the most powerful position in the world. To many, the lesson may be that the end justifies the means and that values

* The devastating recession of 2008–09 was directly linked to the actions of the banking community (and others), who knowingly issued mortgages to unqualified homebuyers with the expectation that the entire process was certain to fail. When it did, the loss was measured in money, jobs and dreams. Of the hundreds of Wall Street bankers, traders and executives who acknowledged being involved in the scandal, only one man—an Egyptian-born employee of Credit Suisse—served prison time. Others waltzed away with profits. Some, such as Jamie Dimon, CEO of JPMorgan Chase, profited greatly. Just weeks after settling charges brought against him by the Justice Department out of court, Dimon received a raise of 74 percent, bringing his annual salary to $20 million.

and principles can be tossed aside if doing so advances your career, consolidates power or bumps up short-term profit levels. That's a sad reflection on American business and society; a dark shadow cast by the country's most powerful leader. Even those in business who may have disagreed with Trump's nomination and campaign style had to recognize that his presidency assumed acceptance of unethical practices among American businesspeople and corporations. This remains a distinct possibility. And a potential tragedy.

An "Unbearable Stench"

American politics has encountered liars in the past. In fact, it's impossible to name any political system, whether it be a free democracy or a benign dictatorship, that has not been directed, influenced, transformed or shaped by men and women to whom the idea of telling the truth is a juvenile fantasy. There is a difference in Trump's outrageous statements, however. Lying presumes at least an awareness of, and interest in, some definition of truth. If a brand of cold cream tells you the product can remove a lifetime's worth of wrinkles overnight, it at least acknowledges the truth about your wishes. The promise may be false, but the goal is true and the effort to convince you is obvious and directed. Trump has no interest in facts, truth, reality or even of convincing anyone of anything. *He doesn't care* about any of that.

Trump goes beyond having an unfamiliarity with facts. He revels in the realm of bullshit, and forgive my use of that term, but the English language does not at the moment have a more elegant phrase to apply in this situation. The degree of B.S. that Trump employs on a regular basis creates, in the words of at least one qualified observer, an "unbearable stench" with almost every phrase he utters and every observation he makes.[7]

So what are the goals of B.S. artists? To generate controversy. To build their own egos. To raise their stature in the minds of those who support them in their own minds. The liar wants to be seen as the one telling the truth; the B.S. artist doesn't care. His or her only goal is to become and remain the center of attention, or to justify some otherwise untenable action or point of view. In these situations, there is neither a role nor a concern for truth. Facts may not matter to B.S. artists, but exaggeration—blended with large portions of outright lies—is pure gold to them. In a rare example of truth and insight, Trump once asked rhetorically, "When did you ever see a sign hanging outside a pizzeria and declaring, 'The fourth-best pizza in the world!'? Never!"[8]

We're not talking pizza here. We are speaking of the acknowledged leader of the free world, the individual duly elected to represent not only the values and aspirations of 330 million Americans but of billions of individuals who view the United States as a guiding light toward happy and fulfilling lives. And what do we give them? A B.S. artist.

So why does he do it? Why does Trump dispense such outrageous statements with no regard for the truth or for his own stature among people whose opinion normally matters? Two reasons.

First, to test the loyalty of his supporters. The best way to learn if anyone is loyal to you is to tell them, or ask them to do, something outrageous.

Second, requiring subordinates to echo and validate outrageous comments and opinions undercuts their independence and solidifies their allegiance. We saw this from the very first day of Trump's presidency, when every member of his staff swore that the crowd of people at his inauguration was larger than the crowd that had attended Barack Obama's, even when photographic evidence proved otherwise. How else can you create that level of devotion? (And: How dangerous and frightening is this blind dedication to a total falsehood when you ponder it with visions of the Nuremberg Rally in your mind?) This is the most disgusting aspect of the stench from Trump's B.S.

But back to business...

The Roots of My Sense of Outrage

The wide application of energy, skill and, in the case of entrepreneurs, money represents the heart of America's success every bit as much as does the beacon of freedom the country has shone across the globe for

250 years. Whenever we risk dimming that beacon, we jeopardize our future and demoralize those who look to this country for guidance. I say this with special fervor and from a specific point of view.

I chose America, I wasn't born here. I came at the invitation of a large corporation, to advance my career. Within a few years of arriving, I determined that America would be more than my home and a place to work; it would be where I could conceive, establish and expand a communications business of my own—one that met my standards of service and principle. And I managed to achieve that ambition. I did it by applying the usual components of business success: a clear vision of my goals, a team of supportive and dedicated employees, and a determination to realize my dream through hard work.

There was another ingredient to this formula. It's as essential as the others but is often in short supply or absent among American business. Many CEOs discount its value or actively dilute its presence in their business practices. For the sake of simplicity, let's call it *integrity*. And let's assume that the term includes the qualities of honesty, truth, fairness and sincerity. Over the thirty-plus years during which I built my business on vision, principles and determination, I reminded myself, and those I employed, of the importance of those qualities. Yes, our primary goal was the building and accumulation of profit through the services we provided—that's the objective of every business venture. But to assume we would score substantial profit levels by bending rules until they shattered in our face was unacceptable, and not on moral grounds alone. I insisted we act with integrity because it would be the basis of trust among everyone with whom we dealt: clients, vendors and the person in the next cubicle. The idea of operating a business in an atmosphere of distrust was not just anathema to me; in my view, it was a recipe for failure.

This book is not my attempt to leverage American business into docility, playing a game in which performance goals are less important than etiquette. Let's be up-front about this: Business is competitive. Business is rough. Business can be stressful. And business demands total attention to achieving whatever goal is set for it. But so does football. And football has rules based on fair play, respect for opponents and officials, and the avoidance of injury. The day that a 300-pound lineman can stomp on a running back's legs or strike a quarterback with a karate chop with impunity will be the day that football becomes a sport no longer. It will also be the day that fans and advertisers leave near-empty stadiums and TV screens blank on autumn Sunday afternoons.

Donald Trump's arrival on the American political scene was like watching an armed platoon of infantrymen march onto a football field and insist that the game be played their way—meaning they would set the rules, do whatever it took to ensure a win, turn their sights on anyone who dared to object, and declare that the only rules that applied were the ones they chose to follow.

I am concerned that the values and actions Donald Trump pursues as President of the United States of America are so empty of scruples and so wide-ranging that they encourage business leaders to toss aside even the weak ethical guidelines in place today. That's the basis of this book: To catalog and castigate the unethical behavior endemic to many American businesses. And to demonstrate that good ethical standards and corporate values don't cost a dime—yet can be cashed for gold.

2

Business Ethics: An Oxymoron That Needn't Be

MANY AMERICANS FIND it difficult to use the words "business" and "ethics" in the same sentence. To them, the phrase sounds like an oxymoron. Which explains why a recent poll[9] revealed that only 17 percent of Americans had a High or Very High opinion of business executives when it comes to honesty and ethics; 32 percent had a Low or Very Low opinion.* Businesspeople could take some solace in the fact that they weren't the lowest-rated profession when it came to honesty and ethics. That dubious distinction belonged to senators (50 percent rated them Low/Very Low) and members of Congress (59 percent rated them Low/Very Low).

Think about this for a moment: The two defining qualities of America that have represented the nation's success and inspired the world's admiration for generations have been our ability to generate wealth to fund a high standard of living and our system of government that provides security and freedom for all citizens. And yet today, our

* If you want respect in America, become a nurse: 84 percent of respondents rated them High/Very High. Or become a pharmacist: they were rated High/Very High for those qualities by 67 percent of respondents.

own people rate our business and government leaders at the very bottom of the list for honesty and integrity. As a measure of the state of the nation in the early years of the twenty-first century, surely this must be alarming. After all, what hope do we have of maintaining all the precious qualities that (forgive me for this phrase) "have made America great" if we cannot trust the people in charge of building and overseeing the economic and legislative engines of the country?

The election of Donald Trump brought the worst aspects of both business and politics to center stage in America. I needn't add my voice to those who decry it as a political catastrophe. My concern is closer to home: I'm sounding the alarm about the extent to which Trump will lower the bar on all the elements of integrity—honesty, ethics and fairness. Tragically, Americans already have such a low opinion of their elected representatives; my fear is that this opinion is about to deteriorate further under the influence of Donald Trump and negatively affect the integrity of business leaders. If this occurs, and America's opinion of business leaders dives to the subterranean levels occupied by members of Congress, the impact will be devastating.

America's success and prosperity have been built on the twin pillars of its political system and its business skills. Respect for our political leaders has sunk in recent years to the point where fewer than one out of five of us trust the federal government.[10] (This, of course, explains at least in part the stunning achievement of Trump winning the presidency based on the fact that he wasn't "an ordinary politician," which was true. Within a few weeks of his inauguration, substantial numbers of Americans wished that he were.) If Trump is assumed to represent the morals and values of American businesspeople generally, we can expect a similar slide in trust and respect for their abilities and achievements.

It goes further than that. Look deeply enough into history and it becomes clear that autocratic regimes that focus on generating wealth and power for themselves do not and cannot maintain the network of trust needed to make any organization run smoothly. The "organization" could be a government, corporation, community, family—your choice. The perception applies equally.

The tactics of schoolyard bullies and the abandonment of traditional ethics in pursuit of maximum profit and power has led to a unique form of chaos—one in which many aspects of community trust and shared concern are not just ignored but are no longer even acknowledged.

Four Measures of Ethics in Business

I'm not a leftist; far from it. Neither was President Eisenhower, but he warned, over half a century ago, of the power of the country's military-industrial complex.* The phrases Eisenhower used in that address—"unwarranted influence" and "the disastrous rise of misplaced power"—revealed his intense concern about American industry's pursuit of profit above all other considerations. Sadly, his warning remains unheeded.

Notwithstanding the example of Donald Trump, the pursuit of profit and a respect for integrity are not mutually exclusive. In fact, as we shall see, making room for both principles and results can catapult almost any business to higher levels of performance. If we permit both business and government to function with little or no concern for honesty and values, can we really expect America to be great? Ever?

In considering the fundamental values and ethics of business and of good government—or the lack of them as demonstrated by Donald Trump—I have chosen to apply four critical metrics that represent qualities we can all recognize and apply:

1. **Accountability:** Acknowledging the impact we have made with our actions, especially when the actions have inflicted damage on some other person or entity.

* "In the councils of government, we must guard against the acquisition of unwarranted influence, whether sought or unsought, by the military-industrial complex. The potential for the disastrous rise of misplaced power exists and will persist. We must never let the weight of this combination endanger our liberties or democratic processes." (John McAdams, "Eisenhower's Farewell Address to the Nation," The Kennedy Assassination. Retrieved January 30, 2017.)

2. **Honesty:** Being truthful in all that we say and do.
3. **Responsibility:** Accepting our role and the role of our organization in contributing to the greater good of the communities in which we operate.
4. **Transparency:** Being as open as possible in the motives behind our decisions and actions.

In drafting these four points, I found myself reflecting on how many of these basic standards I can associate with Donald Trump as either businessman or president. I found none. How many do you find?

Clearly, Donald Trump's occupation of the White House has made a major impact on political concerns and strategies. I'm not even venturing into that arena; it's already crowded with pundits and provocateurs on both sides of the political fence. I'm more concerned about countering the impact of Donald Trump's values on American business. I want to demonstrate that the term "business ethics" is not an oxymoron and that the most successful and admired corporations achieve their status by following ethical business methods, not by ignoring them. The kind of values-based leadership I'm advocating is not just a matter of burnishing a corporate image, raising the public's opinion of businesspeople based on their honesty and integrity. It reaches far deeper and more profoundly than that.

Business in America is not only a means of generating wealth. In many ways it's like life itself: *a cooperative activity dependent upon mutual trust and agreed-upon ethics for its existence and effectiveness*. In a collective manner it is a society of sorts, an association of people and groups whose existence and achievements are interrelated. In that sense it's like any community or neighborhood. No society can survive if its members believe they can lie and steal from each other, breaking promises and agreements whenever they choose. That kind of behavior on a global scale would produce a total breakdown of society, leading to vicious tribal warfare characterized by unrest, uncertainty and instability.

It is not an exaggeration to suppose that a steep decline in American business ethics could trigger a similar drop-off of prosperity and trust among nations. The result could be more than cataclysmic; it could be a disaster that would challenge or even exceed the Great Depression and the two world wars that bookended it.*

Business Decisions: Unpopular or Unethical?

At least some of the low opinion of American business ethics results from the public's inability or refusal to distinguish between actions that are unethical and those that are simply unpopular. It's an important distinction. And it is essential to understand how one is not always linked to the other.

Layoffs and plant closings are a fact of business life. They are unfortunate and tragic to the employees involved, but they are almost always necessary to ensure the viability of a corporation. If laying off a hundred employees will extend the employment of a thousand, the choice becomes obvious even if regrettable. No business executive rejoices over the prospect of putting employees out of a job; most look forward to rehiring them at the earliest opportunity. These kinds of decisions are always unpopular but almost never unethical.

Other business activities may appear unethical on the surface but don't necessarily indicate a lack of principles. For example, offshore sourcing can (although not necessarily) mean that American jobs are lost to foreign workers. Or it may signal that domestic workers are unable or unwilling to assume the same work. There is no better example of this than the presence of migrant farm workers in California's vast agricultural fields. Lost jobs are not always the fault of greedy domestic employers or of illegal immigrant workers. Sometimes

* This isn't an over-the-top observation. Students of history will quickly identify the linkage between the disastrous economic impact on Germany due to reparations the country was forced to pay for its involvement in the Great War (WWI), the resentment deeply felt by the German people, their search for a strong man to lead them, the resultant rise of Nazism and the launch of World War II.

they are the product of our own values and preferences. Again, often unpopular, but not always unethical.

On the other hand, fraud and corruption in business are not merely unethical; they are out-and-out criminal. But public perception tends to group them as a means of doing business; a dangerous misconception perhaps reinforced by some sectors of the media, which often trumpet stories of corrupt behavior by businesspeople. With so much exposure to the misdeeds of corporate leaders, is it any wonder that some people make the leap from knowing that this is unethical behavior to thinking that these are the new norms of business?

The waters are muddied further still when businesspeople take actions that they themselves view as fair, healthy competition but that others may misconstrue as unfair and devious. As long as the public confuses legitimate (if sometimes unpopular) business actions with unethical behavior, it will be difficult to correct the misguided concept that business cannot adhere to ethical conduct and still achieve success.

Competition in business is not something to be condemned. It is something to be celebrated and encouraged when conducted in an environment of fairness and opportunity. The picture admittedly becomes gray at times, as it did when Starbucks launched its initial expansion strategy.

In the 1980s, Starbucks was a small Seattle coffee company whose unique approach changed America's coffee-drinking habit and created an entirely new industry sector. The company's business model was proving correct: Americans would search out and pay a premium price for quality coffee. Once they tasted it, Starbucks customers were no longer content with the liquid that passed for restaurant coffee in those days—usually a bitter day-old brew as similar to good coffee as dishwater is to wine.

The company's objective was to expand so rapidly that competitors would not be able to duplicate its strategy of serving premium-priced coffee in relaxed library-like settings. Starbucks would do this by opening as many outlets as possible in key high-traffic locations, establishing its presence before competitors could react to the market shift. Like all real estate decisions, the three most important aspects in choosing outlet sites were location, location, and location.

Choosing the right spots for new outlets is a crucial step for retailers expanding their chain. Giant retail and food operations such as McDonald's invest millions of dollars searching for the best sites, basing their decisions on detailed (and costly) studies of traffic flow, utilities, access, local income levels and other measures. Starbucks didn't have that kind of money at the time, so it applied an aggressive, even ruthless, approach: essentially, it duplicated the experience of others. The company's search for good sites would involve finding existing operations with a significant number of regular customers—there was no time-and-money-wasting search and investigation into traffic flows and income levels. What Starbucks did was identify existing coffee shops with a large customer base, find an available space nearby and open an outlet there. The location could be across the street or next door; the important thing was to cash in on existing traffic flow and offer a more attractive alternative.

Almost overnight, residents in neighborhoods who patronized an existing restaurant or coffee shop encountered a new source for their java—one that served rich, more consistent coffee in a wide range of flavors. Friendly service, handy tables and comfortable chairs added to the appeal and justified the higher price. The success of Starbucks changed the entire market. Instead of a place to grab hot bitter coffee with meals or drink it on the go, Starbucks was a place to relax with friends over flavorful coffee.

The strategy proved successful. Perhaps no American business in history has expanded as quickly and broadly, and made such a wide impact on one aspect of the American lifestyle. But was it fair? Many people felt it wasn't. They saw Starbucks as an intruder, stealing the loyalty of customers built up over years of service from existing restaurants and coffee shops. This may have been true to a degree, but it wasn't entirely accurate. Starbucks discarded the old way of brewing, serving and marketing coffee. Rather than elbowing restaurants out of the business, it generated a new market and culture based on a better product sold for a premium price in a setting that had not existed in America before. (Coffee shops à la Starbucks had been, of course, part of European culture for centuries.)

So was Starbucks ruthless in its near-predatory expansion strategy, or was it simply practicing good business? I call it good business. Had the existing coffee shops brewed the same marketing mix of product, service and setting, they might have occupied the leading position before Starbucks. It was a matter of concept, timing and competition. In this case, as in most similar instances, the new competitor on the block offered a better product and a more attractive means of providing it to consumers. Starbucks may have been aggressive and hard-nosed in its expansion program, but its actions were not unethical. In fact, Starbucks is a values-driven company that enjoys an enormous amount of goodwill from its customer base precisely because of that approach. Although many American businesspeople choose to operate with little or no regard for ethics, mistakenly sensing that ethics and business don't belong in the same sentence, companies like Starbucks are successful *because* they are astute businesses *and* stick to their principles.

Increasingly for today's organizations, the practice of adhering to a high standard of integrity and respecting key values is essential to their success. Today's consumers respond to stories of unfair treatment and injurious actions at the speed of light—or at least at the speed of Twitter, Facebook and other social media. And the reverse flow is equally swift and powerful. Good news and good business practices travel with precipitous speed over social media; a community of raving fans who feel that your company's business practices are aligned with their values can boost the company's reputation—and results—more effectively than most other strategies you could choose to pursue. Research over several years has revealed that companies rated highly for their ethical standards outperform the average for the U.S. Large Cap Index by 6.6 percent.[11] So it bears repeating: operating a business according to high ethical standards tends to generate higher returns over the long term. Call it a Decency Dividend.

As someone who opposed first the nomination and later the election of Donald Trump, I fear that his election and his actions as president have taken us down the road to accepting and even fostering a business culture that dispenses with values and ethics. None of the least admirable aspects of Trump's business history—from refusing to honor contractual obligations and bragging about using bankruptcies to improve his bottom line[12] to his unlicensed and fraudulent Trump University and blocking all access to information on his business holdings—prevented his election as President of the United States. He is the embodiment of questionable, even unethical, business practices as a means of achieving a measure of success in the corporate world. By hyping his achievements and bragging about the impact of his questionable practices—such as avoiding paying any income tax for several years on an annual income measured in the tens of millions—he confuses the public about what is acceptable and what is not. He subordinates the value and benefits of doing business in a principled way, projecting the image of a shady businessperson perched on a pedestal to be revered. No wonder business leaders and ordinary citizens alike are becoming increasingly confused about what constitutes good business practice and what is unethical and, therefore, unacceptable.

The Best Way to Avoid Harsh Regulations: Behave Ethically

What does this say about America's attitude toward ethics in business? Even for those who chose not to support Trump's election, his success at shrugging off these blemishes on his record entrenched them as acceptable, or at least not worrisome, in the minds of the American public. That is both understandable and tragic. If businessman Donald Trump can flaunt his disdain for so many measures of ethical behavior and still reach the highest office in the land, why should Americans expect more from other businesspeople?

We should, and we must, if for no other reason than to avoid the introduction of complex laws and intrusive investigation to ensure compliance with them. With every new law comes new bureaucracy to enforce it. I'm all for laws, but let's admit it: laws are introduced to ensure that we behave according to a widely accepted level of morality. Their introduction is provoked by actions that society considers harmful and offensive, and they serve to limit future occasions of those actions. They fill an existing need. If American business begins to emulate the low standards of Donald Trump, we can expect either widespread chaos or the introduction of draconian laws—each alternative damaging in its own way.

I know what it's like to deal with complex business regulations. I encountered too many of them when managing my firm's day-to-day operations. Most were like swatting flies with sledgehammers. They were also written by lawyers for other lawyers to interpret, making their creation and enforcement the most effective job-generating device since the rise of trade unions.

Complex regulations are born from government reactions to unacceptable behavior. The best way to make business operations free of new dos and don'ts is for corporations to act in a fair and equitable manner to everyone concerned—employees, vendors, customers and shareholders. It's all a matter of doing the right thing—*and we all know the right thing to do in every situation we encounter*.

That's a simple premise. It's also difficult to expect it to be applied both widely and consistently. Somewhere, sometime, an executive or corporation will choose an unscrupulous path that promises a boost in profits or the avoidance of loss, knowing someone else will be paying the price. Or, when it comes to employee management, that an unfair decision, an insulting remark or some other incident will cast a shadow on their business operations. They will do it and they won't care. Because a standard has been set.

Yes, we need rules, laws, guidelines and regulations. But we don't need more of them. Every new complex government regulation comes with a price tag attached. Businesspeople need to do more than recognize the cost of complying with regulations; they also need to accept that many new laws wouldn't need to be introduced and enforced if business operated in an ethical manner in the first place.

Every new law regulating the conduct of business in America obeys another—the law of unintended consequences. I don't believe state and federal lawmakers consciously search for ways to drain profits from legitimate and law-abiding businesses, but it happens anyway. Virtually all such regulations are a response to unethical actions by American businesses. No better proof of this exists than the Great Recession of 2007–08, which was ignited by sub-prime mortgage practices.

The initial cause of that economic disaster is both so complex and familiar that it needn't require detailing. It's necessary only to recall that everyone involved knew it began with immoral actions taken in pursuit of excessive profits. Had the major participants practiced the most basic ethical guidelines—not falsifying information on mortgage applications, not concealing true borrowing costs, not promoting mortgages to unqualified buyers, and a dozen more—there would have been no Great Recession. And there would be no *Dodd–Frank Wall Street Reform and Consumer Protection Act* of 2010.

In case you haven't read the Act recently—I recommend it as a cure for insomnia—it was created to overhaul America's financial regulatory system on a major scale. The goal was to avoid a recurrence of the events in 2007–08. It took the U.S. Congress sixty-seven studies, twenty-two periodic reports, 243 separate rules and eventually a dozen or so new agencies to do it. The new agencies included the Financial Stability Oversight Council, the Office of Financial Research and the Bureau of Consumer Financial Protection.

No one seems prepared to estimate the direct cost to taxpayers for designing and implementing the Act. Whatever they are, the totals may well be dwarfed by indirect hidden costs to banks and individuals. The legislation requires banks to establish compliance teams and programs, producing a hit on bank profits, especially for smaller regional operations. The response of these locally important banks was to absorb the losses by cutting back on customer benefits such as free checking. The people at the root of the financial crisis made uncalculated millions. And the bill for those millions was paid, whether they recognized it or not, by American taxpayers. The impact didn't end there. When it became clear that the Act enabled consumers to sue lenders for misjudging their ability to repay loans, some lenders pulled out of the mortgage business entirely.[13]

The Great Recession was no inconsequential fly, but, as I noted earlier, regulatory responses by governments tend to resemble sledgehammers more than swatters, and *Dodd-Frank* was no different. The resulting collateral damage was inflicted not on the giant financial institutions that played the most villainous roles in the game but on small regional banks and eventually every American citizen. According to one study, the share of American banking assets held by smaller community banks was cut in half between 1994 and 2014. Much of the drop was attributed to the impact of the *Dodd-Frank Act*.[14]

How's that for irony? Unscrupulous mortgage lenders harvest untold millions in sub-prime mortgages, giant international financial institutions peddle them for billions in profits, the U.S. federal government responds with draconian measures... and who pays the bills? Taxpayers and small community banks.*

I don't want more of these convoluted regulatory acts and nor does anyone else, with the exception of heavyweight corporate and tax lawyers. Let me repeat: Regulations don't breed on their own. They're spawned by businesspeople who refuse to follow the golden rules they were first taught in kindergarten: play fair, tell the truth, don't be greedy, and treat everyone else the way you want them to treat you.

From Sledgehammers to Swords

If many of the laws created to regulate American businesses resemble sledgehammers, the growing alternative is something of a double-edged sword thanks to the power of social media, which I mentioned earlier. Swung in one direction, it can effectively overwhelm competitors and boost a business. Swung the other way, and the offending corporation finds itself struggling to maintain its balance and credibility.

* In June 2017, Congress chose to repeal most *Dodd-Frank* measures, eliminating the Orderly Liquidation Authority, which allows the federal government to step in if a bank is near collapse to ensure the institution's failure would not spread to the rest of the financial system. Senator Elizabeth Warren, a fierce critic of Wall Street, called the bill a "hand-out to Wall Street."

Social media communicates tales of unethical business behavior with lightning efficiency. It may take weeks for a single unethical act to be detected by the authorities, months to investigate it and file charges, and years to pursue it in court. Not so, of course, if the unscrupulous action becomes notorious on Facebook, Twitter and the herds of blogs and other cyber activities. Operating 24-7 and communicating with their followers at or near the speed of light, social media vehicles have convinced American business to ignore them at their peril.

Walmart got the message in 2012 when the company tried to cover up bribery practices in Mexico. In one instance, its Mexican subsidiary slipped $32,000 to a Mexican government official, paid to delay a zoning decision. The delay would enable Walmart to receive approval for a new retail outlet that the community had opposed, sneaking approval under the wire. It's the kind of move that not only gives businesspeople a reputation for operating without regard for community concerns but also demonstrates a complete rejection of ethics. Walmart executives denied the charge, which proved deceitful when the *New York Times* launched an investigation, confirmed the story was true and went on to expose a pattern of bribery through much of Walmart Mexico's operations.[15]

What began as a black eye for Walmart 's claim of acting ethically where customers and suppliers were concerned became a public thrashing when waves of tweets, blogs and other Internet-based condemnation broke on its shores. Walmart backed down and local laws, we can assume, have been followed from that day forward. But the PR damage was done, not just to Walmart but to American business generally.*

It's not all bad news and negative results. Many firms, including some of America's largest corporations, have learned to make use of social media with positive results. Ford Motor Company is one. Its

* To be fair, the improper actions may have been limited to Walmart's Mexico operations. As we'll see in Chapter 18, Warren Buffett's trust in the integrity of the company was substantial in at least one massive transaction between the retailer and Buffett's Berkshire Hathaway firm. The Mexican episode demonstrates, however, how unethical conduct by one division can taint an entire corporation.

blog, *The Ford Story*, invites Ford owners to share tales of their cars, including comments on design and performance. This may sound risky, but it has actually paid off by positioning Ford as a company that seeks to connect with its customers.* Reportedly, Ford has also gleaned some design ideas from the site. And for several years now, various national brands such as Whole Foods, Starbucks, Southwest Airlines and Marriott International have employed Twitter sites to capitalize on their direct relationships with their customers.

Is it worth the effort of your company opening up through social media, not to mention the risk of having large numbers of people trash you and your product? I say it is, because it demonstrates that you are confident enough in the integrity of your business to accept the odd brickbat and employ it to your advantage. Besides, customers and others are going to talk about you on social media anyway, whether you encourage it or not, so you may as well participate in an effort to engage them more closely.

Consumers want to be heard. They want to express their opinion and, more than that, they want to connect with companies that appear open and up-front in their dealings. Is it too far a reach to suggest that these companies make gains in reputation and currency because they appear to act decently when it comes to dealing with individuals, and that this quality can boost levels of brand loyalty?

No, it is not. Far from being an oxymoron, "business" and "ethics" can and should go hand in hand. As social media responses to values-based companies reveal, not only is good corporate behavior good business, it can be a key factor in vaulting an organization into new levels of customer engagement and loyalty—paying rich dividends in enhanced goodwill, reputation and overall performance.

* To be sure, Ford may have learned its lesson about customer relationships as a result of twin disasters involving the company's Explorer SUV and compact Pinto automobile, detailed in chapters 3 and 4.

3

Measures of Integrity

All systems—political, economic, social or justice—tend to be dominated by strong personalities. Every American with a minimum level of awareness and understanding can (or should be able to) link the essence of any given system with an individual or group of individuals who represent its values. The choice may vary; your idea of a dominant personality in American jurisprudence, for example, could be Judge Billings Learned Hand or Oliver Wendell Holmes, while mine might be Earl Warren. The rule still holds.

Individuals play a leading role in the stories we tell ourselves to clarify our vision of the world around us. Their character and actions interpret the way a system works and help define our role within it. The focus remains on people, real and imagined. We grow intrigued by their persona, enthralled by their adventures and influenced by who they are and what they represent. Some inspire us to emulate their values and achievements; others repel us by their immoral actions and lack of human values. Most of us, knowingly or unknowingly, place a great deal of emphasis on charismatic leadership, holding individual leaders up as our role models, whatever their measure and abilities. In America, the focus on charismatic leadership goes well beyond that of almost all other countries, often assessing an individual's accomplishments and appeal based on materialistic success. It appears we can forgive much if someone in a position of power or status has amassed great wealth without being convicted of a crime in the process.

When it comes to business and economics, think of the contrasting roles played by characters such as Bernie Madoff and Warren Buffett. Or Bill Gates and Gordon Gecko; Andrew Carnegie and Booker T. Washington; Katharine Graham and Ray Kroc. What does each pairing tell you about values, ideals and the pride you take in calling yourself an American? The rule still holds: We look to those in power as guidelines for our behavior, our values and our distinction. We don't always model them, and in many cases, we may distance ourselves from them.

To an enormous number of our citizens, the ultimate American role model and position is the one at the pinnacle of power in this country: the occupant of the White House. Donald Trump, like every U.S. president before him, thus wields tremendous influence on the thinking and conduct of others. His impact has been enormous. And damaging. Trump's position as POTUS, and the immense power that comes with it, commands respect for the office he holds but also draws attention to his less-than-redeeming qualities and antics. He is perpetually aware of this attention-getting aspect of every action he takes and every utterance he makes. Unfortunately, he is either unaware of, or indifferent to, the negative impact of what he says and does—not on his image, which he carefully molds and shapes, but on the wider actions and mores of American society.

I call it "Trump creep"—the constant chipping away at decency, at what is socially acceptable and at the truth, in favor of the sweeping use of invectives against individuals and organizations in response to even the smallest criticism. True, some of this kind of behavior has been fostered by the rise of social media and the anonymity it affords people to make caustic and disgusting personal comments to strangers whose only fault was to make a mild observation. Social media, as one observer noted, "has normalized casual cruelty."[16] It has also, let's face it, made the corrosive comments mouthed by Donald Trump more acceptable to a substantial number of citizens. Can we honestly suggest that his lack of integrity has had any less effect?

Whether Trump's ease at telling falsehoods and abandonment of widely accepted moral values is cause or effect doesn't matter. He does things that I and others find repulsive and at odds with the standards we value. The impact of his actions on American ethical standards will surely be destructive and lasting, precisely because of his position of power.

Defining Business Ethics—Easy or Impossible?

Most of us have a good idea of the definition of ethics. We equate them with fairness, morality, honesty and other qualities associated with goodness. I suggest we be more specific where individuals are concerned. I propose this for a start: *Ethics are the set of moral principles that guide a person's behavior.*

That sounds fine. It breaks down, however, when you try applying it to much of American business today. Too many businesspeople are guided not by ethics but by compliance. They're not concerned about doing what they know is best for everyone involved; they're concerned with measuring how much they can get away with before the cost, in fines or loss of reputation, becomes too heavy.

Over and over again, you and I witness companies investing time, effort and money into reducing fines levied as a result of them committing infractions *instead of behaving in a manner that would have prevented them from incurring the fines in the first place.* Corporate legal counselors are well-schooled and often well-experienced in details such as federal sentencing and economic penalty precedents, *but they cannot end unethical practices in their companies.* And, I suspect, they rarely attempt to do so.

Ethics are not measured in words, they are measured in deeds. In business they can be put into practice only if they are driven by the principles and values of owners and executives who weigh the legitimate pursuit of profit against the greater cost to the community. Values-based leadership is business ethics in action, the moral compass of an organization that guides every decision made and every action taken according to the perhaps nebulous but always understood criterion of "doing the right thing." *And we always know the right thing to do.*

Donald Trump appears to reject any notion of doing the right thing if it fails to enhance either his earnings or his ego. From declaring multiple bankruptcies while ignoring their impact on partners, employees, suppliers and shareholders; to concealing his income tax returns and walking away from failed and apparently fraudulent business ventures such as Trump University, Trump Airlines, Trump Mortgage and Trump Steaks*, the man's actions have been weighed only according to whatever benefit they afforded him personally.

Let's be clear: On their own, business failures do not indicate an absence of ethics. But the circumstances surrounding so many of Trump's failed companies—such as his overhyped Trump University, for which he paid $25 million to settle claims from disgruntled fraud victims—suggest that the only thing guiding Trump in the venture was another way to maximize his profits with minimal concern for others.

Presidential Style and Men's Hats

We cannot escape the influence of those occupying high positions in government and business, because they occupy a similar place in our consciousness. Much of what they say and do makes an impact on the way we conduct our lives. Sometimes their influence is relatively minor in the grand scheme of things but instructive in the way we model our behavior on theirs. Here's a good example:

Look at men pictured in photographs and movies through the first half of the twentieth century. Until 1960, nearly every adult male in

* The steaks were promoted as being identical to those served at the "DTJ" Steak House in Las Vegas, and the company collapsed soon after the restaurant was closed in 2012 for fifty-one health code violations.

America wore a hat. To men of almost every rank, a proper hat was as important to a wardrobe as shoes. Men wouldn't think of leaving home without a hat. Laborers and blue-collar workers wore cloth caps. Businessmen chose a fedora when sporting a suit and tie. For formal occasions, such as the inauguration of a new American president, top hats were the style (stovepipe-looking accessories whose only practical function appeared to be to serve as targets for schoolchildren armed with snowballs). But after 1961, hats became as rare on the heads of American men as lampshades. The reason? John F. Kennedy was elected president the previous year. Kennedy disliked wearing hats and dispensed with them. Soon, so did most American men. Now think of Donald Trump. Business ethics are not hats, I agree. (And, if I need point out, Donald Trump is no JFK.) But the effect holds true. As I write this, America has a leader whose values are almost entirely at odds with those of the majority of U.S. citizens. Yet he occupies a position that represents a model of behavior for all of us. The high profile of his presidency serves as a paradigm, a guideline we feel obligated to accept and perhaps follow.

Speaking psychologically, much of our response is unconscious. Few men in the early 1960s thought to themselves, "Gee, Kennedy doesn't wear a hat, so I guess I won't either." Their minds began shifting away from tradition toward an unaware mimicking of the much-admired young president's behavior. They were influenced by Kennedy's fashion sense even when it conflicted with their customary behavior, because "what is good enough for the president..."

The point, of course, is not whether JFK preferred to wear a hat, it's that we don't always consciously choose to follow an influential person's behavior. We are naturally and sometimes unwittingly drawn into the orbit of a charismatic leader, and we fall into step while following along. It's not heel-clicking blind obedience. It's a matter of assuming that, in this case, the leader of a country that has signified freedom to much of the rest of the world for more than two centuries represents a standard of behavior for citizens everywhere—especially those who call themselves Americans. We choose our leaders partly because we believe their goals and values are aligned with our own. Or at least we used to. Today, even if no one or only few are choosing to act like Trump, America's standard of behavior risks slipping because of his influence.

I've already spoken about the dangers of our business leaders following Trump's tarnished example, choosing to pursue profit and personal wealth while dispensing with traditional values. There is, in turn, a greater, more widespread danger of the people in business leaders' organizations unquestioningly following them. Isn't it the responsibility of all leaders to consider their influence on those whom they lead, and to model behavior worthy of being emulated?

Why Can't Both Sides Benefit?

Donald Trump has never attempted to disguise his biases, his warped sense of values and his inability to behave in a generous and charitable manner. After declaring his plans to seek the presidency, when asked about his qualifications for being the U.S. president and commander in chief his sole response was, "I beat people. I win."[17] That's an admirable reply for a football coach, quiz show contestant or battlefield commander, but business is none of those. Nor should it be.

The intent of Starbucks' aggressive expansion policy, which I mentioned earlier, was not to annihilate every coffee house and restaurant in the country. Nor should it have been. Total dominance of any market, leaving the victor free of competition, is unhealthy. This applies whether the business involves selling coffee, building hotels or governing a nation.

The success of Starbucks prompted Americans to drink more coffee, pay a higher price for the enjoyment and demand similar standards from other sources. The company's success changed the habits of consumers and expanded the market to make room for similar operations. That's how business works. The notion of business as mortal combat in which one side wins totally and the other loses unconditionally is both foolish and flawed. Nobel Prize–winning economist Milton Friedman's *Capitalism and Freedom*, written more than a half century ago, emphasized that successful business transactions benefit both parties "provided (that) the transaction is bilaterally voluntary and informed."[18] Friedman painted an image of an ideal commercial exchange that stressed a concept of trade conducted within a civil transaction mutually benefiting both sides. Nothing in Friedman's concept extolled bankruptcies (Trump has taken this route four times in his business career, representing write-offs by suppliers, vendors and employees totaling in the hundreds of millions of dollars) or the application of raw power in economic transactions.

Friedman's views were enlightening, but they were not entirely original. More than two hundred years earlier, Adam Smith wrestled with the question of equating the self-interest of capitalism with the social demands of polite society. The obvious solution, Smith suggested, was cooperation between all sides in business transactions. Going beyond simple economics, Smith saw the daily engagement of businesspeople as a means of building trust, achieving common purposes and generating mutual understanding.

You may see these positions as elements of ancient history. Or, to put it in the vernacular of Donald Trump, the philosophy of losers. They are neither. In a world that continues to accelerate in so many spheres—technically, socially, scientifically—we desperately need touchstones of trust to provide stability. Without them, we sense that we are losing control of our lives, and that our smallest decisions are dictated to us by powers far removed from us that have somehow wrestled away control of our destiny.

Trump attributes all of the challenges faced by America either to enemies beyond its borders or to domestic insurgents whose loyalty is questionable and whose goals are traitorous. His appeal is direct, simplified and shallow. Those who resent paying an exorbitant price for a coffee in an airport because they are within the security zone will fix the blame on foreign terrorists. Others will scowl when they visit kiosks for payday loans, paying interest rates considered usurious and criminal under any other circumstances. Their anger will not be directed at the grasping operators of the business; it will be aimed at individuals and organizations whose actions and policies are somehow responsible for the apparent decline of America—a decline that, thanks to the extremist wings of American society, afflicts them directly. They have lost trust—in the future, in their country, in their community, and in the traditional guidelines that steered Americans for generations. The implications of a serious loss of trust within a society are troubling.

Widespread loss of trust creates an assortment of problems in any society. On a business level, it belies Friedman's proposition that both parties in a transaction benefit when the deal is voluntary and conducted by equally informed associates. On a political level, it sows the opinion that only a strong man, a Donald Trump, a leader with near-absolute powers and a goal of total victory, can free average citizens from unfair dominance. Like the wolf can free the sheep from the tyranny of the farmer.

Of Course, Profit Matters

Based on interviews, quotes, Tweets, books, his multiple bankruptcies and principally his actions, Donald Trump's model for each commercial exchange is, in the words of John Paul Rollert, "a small battle in a never-ending war for financial supremacy."[19]

Virtually every aspect of Trump's actions, speeches and scribblings has promoted the concept that the route to success in business involves targeting weakness, exploiting frailty and taking advantage of naïveté. Rollert described the outcome of actions and values such as these as follows: "A world of ruthless competitors guided by nothing more than blind ambition for profit is hardly a pleasant place."[20]

Personal or professional success in business does not demand this kind of behavior. More than that, it mustn't. Business in a democracy does not function in a vacuum of ethics. It acts as a vital weave in the fabric of society, shaping the mutual exchange of benefit that we talked about earlier.

It is not naive to suggest the goal of business is not exclusively about making enormous volumes of profit. It is simply realistic. Profit matters, of course. Always has, always will. But it is ultimately foolish and self-limiting to assume that business can generate maximum profitability only by dispensing with respect for large numbers of the people it affects. Businesses function within communities. And in many ways, individual businesses shape themselves as unique communities whose members include employees, partners, suppliers, customers, shareholders and other stakeholders. They interact with other communities beyond their own walls and, ultimately, with the social, economic and geographic communities surrounding them. The degree varies, but every component of these wider communities depends on the others economically, socially and environmentally. Proposing that a business operation has an obligation to make a positive influence on its surroundings by assuming a positive role in the economic and social welfare of the community is not socialist. It is simply (wait for it) good business. It pays dividends many times over in satisfied employees and customers, growth and sustainable profits—and in improved performance overall.

Any commercial operation whose guiding philosophies are, conversely, in line with those of Donald Trump cannot expect to harvest the benefits of long-lasting relationships. The people who advocate this kind of action are like midway barkers from my childhood who promised my friends and me incredible sights inside the carnival tent. We paid the admission and were fooled, but that was part of the game. The barkers planned to take our money and never see us again—at least not until the carnival passed through the town the next year.

Unless you prefer a carnival midway to a thriving community and nation, you want business to function within an accepted standard of ethical behavior. This involves living up to a handful of measures of integrity that are easy to recognize, appreciate and understand. They are also not difficult to implement. Based on his actions so far, few appear to be part of Trump's approach to business.

HONESTY

Honesty in business involves applying standards to everything from accounting procedures to ensuring that your product or service performs the way your customers expect. It must go beyond that, however, to apply equally to boardroom decisions, where questionable ethics too often reign. Some of the most infuriating examples of dishonesty in business involve publicly traded companies who reward top executives according to the impact of their decisions on the firm's share price, usually measured quarterly. If quarterly profits meet or exceed a target level and the company's share price climbs accordingly, the execs pocket fat bonuses in the form of stock options and other perks.

On paper it's a fine incentive. In practice, ethics can be tossed aside in the interest of inflating quarterly profit statements. This can be achieved in various ways, including the timing of key contract completions, the sales of assets to conceal losses, and using lies justified by phrases like "industry standards," "legal requirements" and other mealymouthed excuses. Like blueberries.

I love blueberries. Most people do. And most people know that blueberries deliver a wide range of health benefits in the bargain. When we read "blueberries" in the product name and see them in photographs on the package, we believe we'll be enjoying real blueberries. We're usually not. Instead of blueberries, you'll probably consume a mixture of sugar, corn cereal, modified food starch, partially hydrogenated vegetable oil, artificial flavor, cellulose gum, salt and some shade of blue dye.

Okay, truth in packaging has never represented a pillar of business integrity in America. We have become cynical about discovering the truth in the foods we eat, which proves my point. When this degree of cynicism is matched elsewhere in business, on more critical concerns than fictional berries in our pastries and cereal, we will have slipped several levels in trust.

From time to time, an American business not only decides to be honest, but quickly converts its honesty into a benefit. The most famous of these is probably Avis who, back in the 1960s, admitted that its major rival, Hertz, was the largest rental car company in the country. So Avis declared, "We're only #2. So we try harder." Such openness and honesty was unheard of. It was also effective: within the first year of the campaign Avis's share of the market rose by 28 percent.[21] How's that for a dividend?

Of course, every corporation needs to grow; competitive free-enterprise environments dictate that a lack of growth leads to imminent death. The challenge is to grow without distorting the true picture of the company's health. It can be done. It *has* been done by America's most eminent companies. And it *must* be done to maintain confidence in the country's business operations.

FAIRNESS

Being fair is part of being honest, of course, but fairness is something of a gray area rather than a fixed set of guidelines. It may be hard to define absolutely what is fair and what is not, but we all know fairness when we see it... and we begin to lose faith when it's nowhere to be seen at all. For example, some employees and staff members may be treated differently from others. Is it fair to award a top sales performer with a perk that's not available to others in the company? Perhaps. Is it fair to conceal this practice from everyone? No.

I have always believed that there are no degrees of honesty, which makes it easy to define—you are either honest or you are not. You are either fair or not fair in your dealings as a businessperson as well, but defining the term is a little less clear-cut. So here are my definitions of fairness, which I believe can stand up to scrutiny:

1. Making decisions based on appropriate criteria, avoiding favoritism or prejudice.
2. Treating everyone according to their abilities and merit.
3. Correcting mistakes and misdeeds quickly and effectively.
4. Avoiding blaming or punishing someone whose actions were honest and well-intentioned, while taking suitable action against violators of laws and moral obligations.
5. Refusing to take unfair advantage of someone's error or ignorance.
6. Considering and respecting the rights and points of view of others who may disagree with your opinion, giving them the opportunity to clarify their position.

Fairness is all about respect—for others, for diverse perspectives, for principles and standards, and for doing what is right.

SERVICE IN THE BEST INTERESTS OF OTHERS

A business may be many things, but it is not, and should not be, a charity. But this doesn't make the pursuit of profit the exclusive concern, especially the short-term "Let's kick the quarterly report over the moon!" approach that has become common with publicly traded companies. Donald Trump is famed for insisting that business must be a zero-sum game. The concept of both sides of a business transaction benefiting is alien to him.

Of course, tough decisions must be made from time to time that create problems for various stakeholders. Individual dismissals, or broader layoffs and plant closures, for example, are difficult for any business, but they are not personal and need not be driven by entirely negative motivations. Cutting hundreds of jobs helps to cut costs and improve profitability, but sometimes sacrificing a limited number of employees can help to save thousands of jobs, or even the company itself. Making business decisions with the best interests of everyone in mind is the mark of brilliant and, ultimately, successful executives.

Keeping the interests of others in mind can extend beyond the walls of the business itself, to the broader community. When two large pharmaceutical firms, Ciba-Geigy and Sandoz Laboratories, merged to form Novartis in 1996, the new CEO introduced the idea of a global Community Partnership Day, an event that would both unify the new company and express its concern for communities on a worldwide scale. Each subsidiary was asked to choose a local cause it would support and assign one working day for its employees, at all levels, to volunteer their services. The impact has been enormous. In 2017, Novartis employees numbered almost 120,000 in fifty-two countries, each encouraged to, in the words of the company, "leverage their strengths and skills to deliver on our mission of discovering new ways to improve and extend people's lives."

On May 11, 2017, more than 4,500 Novartis associates in the United States took that day—a working day, not a weekend—to volunteer at elementary schools, libraries, soup kitchens, women's shelters and senior citizen residences. Imagine, an entire day of production and selling sacrificed to assist needy groups in communities across the world. What would Donald Trump think of that?

Whatever he might think, it would pale alongside the growth and overall success of Novartis over the years since the Community Partnership Day was launched. Depending on how you measure it, Novartis is either the largest or the second-largest pharmaceutical firm in the world, with an annual revenue of $48.5 billion from assets of more than $130 billion.[22]

CONSISTENCY

Customers want to know what to expect from a business. When a business delivers inconsistences in product quality or customer service, its customers grow anxious or dissatisfied and take their business elsewhere. If I receive a free service from my bank today, and am charged two dollars for the same service next week, the resentment I feel will far exceed the pain of paying a couple of bucks. I'll wonder what I did or didn't do this time that changed things.

Inconsistency in business breeds uncertainty, and uncertainty makes it difficult to build trust. It's not always about money. If one employee treats me like a valued customer today and the next person I encounter acts as though I am an unwanted intrusion in his life, what's my response? I'll likely forget how good I felt about the first experience and assume that my business is unwanted.

My response may be based more on emotion than on logic. But no one should assume that a negative emotional response to a business transaction is unimportant. Customers want to know what to expect from a business, whether the transaction involves ice cream treats or new cars. Companies that maintain high ethics find ways to deliver consistent helpful service. They also find ways to be consistent in their dealings with employees and suppliers. Without consistency all three groups grow unsure of what to expect. So they usually expect the worst.

OPENNESS

Success in business depends a good deal on confidentiality. Proprietary information and marketing strategy cannot be made available to whoever asks for them. So should businesses be run like the CIA? No, they can't. The CIA, after all, does not attract customers. Nor is it concerned with customer loyalty. Businesses need to establish and maintain the appropriate degree of openness with customers as well as with employees and other stakeholders.

All of the groups I referred to earlier—customers, employees, suppliers and shareholders—have a reasonable right to know about aspects of a business that have a major impact on them, such as product defects and substantial changes in company policy. Dealing with these concerns may be complex but it is agonizing to deal with the fallout if truth is first concealed and later dramatically revealed or, worse, exposed by the press or social media. Transparency, where appropriate, can do far more than avoid short-term pain; sometimes it can generate long-term dividends.

The classic example of the dividends of openness and ethical behavior involves Tylenol, one of the country's most popular medications for pain relief. In 1982, when seven people in Chicago died as a result of taking cyanide-infused Extra Strength Tylenol capsules, the parent company, Johnson & Johnson, faced an unprecedented crisis. How could trust in the brand be restored? And what could Johnson & Johnson say to reduce the impact of people dying from a medication they expected would help them? What Johnson & Johnson said is not important. What they did made all the difference.

Johnson & Johnson launched an immediate recall of every container of Tylenol in North America, a move that cost them over $100 million (in 1982 dollars) at retail. The company shut down the Tylenol production line, suspended advertising for the product and set to work developing tamper-proof packaging that became a standard for similar consumer products. One alleged advertising "genius" claimed that Johnson & Johnson would never sell another product under the Tylenol name.[23]

He was wrong. American consumers were so impressed with the openness of Johnson & Johnson that Tylenol soon regained its market share. More than thirty-five years later, it remains a dominant over-the-counter brand for pain relief. Its post-crisis success was wholly attributed to the open and honest attitude of the manufacturer.*

Good PR? Yes, but it was more than that. No public relations program could possibly have succeeded on its own without Johnson & Johnson accepting complete responsibility as the manufacturer and being totally open about its response. That's one of the lessons of the incident: Tylenol didn't need a PR strategy. It used openness and honesty instead.

Too often, businesspeople assume the best way to deal with a serious problem is not to talk about it—even when multiple fatalities are involved. Which usually leads to a problem much bigger and more damaging. One such mishap led to the demise of both a business and a personal relationship between two of the most esteemed families in American business. If Tylenol was a model of how to deal with a crisis openly and honestly, this was an example of how to destroy two corporate reputations with one disastrous response to tragedy.

The families were Ford and Firestone. Henry Ford and Harvey Firestone became friends at the dawn of the automotive industry, supporting each other while guiding the development of the automobile from a curiosity to the basis of the American economy. Each partner encouraged and assisted the other. Through the twentieth century, a Ford vehicle shipped from the factory without Firestone tires was rarer than a four-leaf clover.

The association remained strong even after Firestone became a subsidiary of the Japanese tire giant Bridgestone in 1988. Two years later, Ford introduced its Explorer SUV, and that's when things began to disintegrate, starting with its Firestone tires. During preproduction testing, Ford engineers had observed that the Explorer tended to roll over easily due to its relatively high center of gravity. If this were the case,† the obvious solution was a total redesign of its suspension

* While various suspects were named during the criminal investigation, no one was ever convicted of essentially murdering the seven people who died as a result of taking the cyanide capsules disguised to look like Tylenol.

† Later investigation suggested that the vehicle was no more likely to roll over than competitive SUVs of its era.

system. The cost would be in the millions and could delay introduction of the Explorer by two years or more. But it would have been the honest and open thing to do.

Instead of honesty and openness, Ford took an easier route. Firestone had recommended 35 psi on tires for the Explorer; Ford insisted on 26 psi and urged Firestone to agree with this figure. The reduced pressure lowered the height of the Explorer a tiny amount and along with the "mushiness" of the softer tires, Ford believed, the chances of a rollover would be reduced. More important, it would save the company large sums of money. The softer tires raised the Explorer's fuel consumption, however, so Ford asked Firestone to build a lighter version of the same tire. Somehow Firestone managed to do so, but the move raised questions about the tire's strength.

Explorer owners soon became involved in serious and often fatal accidents resulting from the catastrophic failure of the Firestone tires. Lowering the pressure levels meant the tires ran hot at highway speeds—much hotter than planned when the tires were originally designed. This caused many of the tires to shred their treads at speeds of over fifty miles per hour, resulting in highway deaths and serious injuries numbering in the hundreds.

At first, both sides denied a problem existed. The cause, they claimed, was poor driving habits or bad weather. When Congress held hearings on the matter, representatives of Ford and Firestone acted like schoolyard children, each pointing to the other and crying, "He started it!" Everyone lost—both companies suffered a major drop in buyer confidence. Firestone's credibility dropped so far that the brand was in danger of extinction. Between lawsuits and product recalls, the total monetary damage easily exceeded a billion dollars. And there were those reported 300-plus deaths and serious injuries.

Imagine what would have happened—or *not* happened—had Ford delayed launching the Explorer until its suspension and handling problems were solved.* Or if Firestone had not agreed that the lower psi was acceptable. In essence, things would have been much different

* Ford's "all-new Explorer" introduced in 2002 boasted suspension design improvements that Ford management had rejected years earlier as too costly.

if each side had done the right thing and put an accepted level of ethical behavior ahead of their quest for maximum profits.

Another example of being open and honest when disaster strikes: Listeriosis is a serious form of food poisoning, and when the bacterium causing the illness was found in processed meats produced at one plant of a large Canadian food company, it proved a major crisis. The company, Maple Leaf Foods, responded in textbook fashion: all of its packaged meat products were recalled and destroyed, and every square inch of the entire plant—a massive facility producing over two hundred different products—was totally disinfected under the watchful eye of microbiologists called in to supervise the effort. By this time an untold number of people who had consumed the product fell ill, and as many as twenty died from its effects. More had to be done, or the company's credibility and future operations would never recover.

The significant point of this tragedy is that when Maple Leaf executives consulted their lawyers and listened to the advice they offered—they rejected it. The lawyer suggested looking for ways to shift the blame, or at least share it, with others. Food inspectors, machinery manufacturers, maintenance firms, doctors and others, the legal professionals suggested, could all have played a part. Find a way to deflect some of the responsibility their way.

One thing the lawyers advised Maple Leaf Foods not to do was apologize. Yet that's exactly what they did, avoiding wordsmiths, spin doctors or bobbing and weaving. The company CEO apologized in TV commercials and on YouTube, saying, "Going through the crisis there are two advisers I've paid no attention to. The first are the lawyers and the second are the accountants."

Those familiar with the situation faced by Maple Leaf Foods generally agree that its openness and candor in the face of such a tragedy saved the company. Despite the PR disaster, the company recovered quickly and has prospered over the years since.

LET'S PUT ALL of these aspects of integrity in perspective. They extend beyond business and politics, and can be summed up in a single short familiar word: Trust.

Nothing we achieve, nothing we aspire to and nothing we value in our hearts can exist without trust. If this sounds a little Sunday School in nature, that's understandable because it is so basic to our lives. Every act, by us as individuals and by corporations as economic entities, must operate on a foundation of trust if it hopes to succeed.

It would be reasonable to expect that an individual capable of achieving the height of political success that Donald Trump has enjoyed would recognize the benefits of building trust among the people he represents as president. But he attained office in the same manner that he achieved so much of his financial success—on the basis of promises that he too often failed to keep and an uneasy relationship with the truth. Along the way, he has squandered much of the trust that Americans, including those who chose to support him, granted him.

We can learn to withhold our trust in Trump. But how much trust can we grant businesspeople—especially those who believe that he may hold the key to their future prosperity?

4

How the Pursuit of Profit Can Make You Blind—and Maybe Deaf as Well

I HAVE A THEORY about successful businesspeople. I believe they are all, to some extent, amateur psychologists.

That will come as a surprise to many of them. Business, they might respond, is all about valuation, investment, opportunity, economic conditions and at least a dozen other considerations—not to mention vision, focus and hard work. Lots of hard work.

I agree. But behind all the decisions that business leaders make is a sense of how people will react to the product and service being offered. Good managers also need to understand how their employees respond to decisions, guidelines and values within an organization. We are all individuals, it's true. But we are all human, after all, and so we respond in similar ways to many situations. That's the specialty of psychologists, and any businessperson who believes that he or she won't benefit from some basic psychological insight is fooling himself or herself.

Obviously, I'm no psychologist, but like so many other people who have built a business of some size and substance literally from the ground up, I have some understanding of the way people react in certain situations. One key study confirmed my instincts about human behavior, even when it seemed at odds with good sense or even basic values. Known as The Milgram Experiment, it was named for the Yale University psychologist who conducted it back in 1961. You may have heard of it even if your interest in psychology equals your interest in quantum physics. If the details are familiar to you, they are still a lesson worth reflecting on.

Stanley Milgram was curious about how far people would go if they were instructed by an authority figure who assured them that their actions were deemed acceptable and correct. Three months before he conducted the experiment, the trial of German Nazi war criminal Adolf Eichmann had begun. Eichmann was charged with playing a major role in the murder of millions of Jews and others whom the Nazis had labeled "undesirables." His defense, offered by so many others before him, was that he had been following orders. Those above him, in positions of authority, had commanded him to slaughter innocent people and assured him, in so many words, that it was "the right thing to do."

Really? The rest of the world wondered about that. How could any civilized, thinking human being take part in such an act, and on such a scale? Milgram wondered about this as well, and he set up his experiment at Yale to explore it.

The Scary Side of Psychology

The experiment involved three people: the Experimenter, supposedly a member of the Yale faculty who played the authoritative role; the Learner, whose response to the experiment would determine the findings; and the Teacher, who was to quiz the Learner and provide either reward or punishment as needed. Both the Experimenter and the Learner understood what was going on. The Teachers (the experiment was repeated several times with different volunteers* playing

* Volunteers were paid $4 per hour for their participation.

the Teacher role) assumed that the Learner was a volunteer and that everything that was about to happen was real.

The experiment involved the Teacher asking the Learner a long series of questions based on word linkages. The Teacher and Experimenter sat in one booth; the Learner was in another booth out of sight. Teacher and Learner were introduced to each other before things began. The Teacher noted that the Learner was strapped into a chair ("So he cannot escape," the Experimenter explained) and was wired to what appeared to be an electric transformer. It was explained that the goal was to measure how much better the Learner would get at coming up with the correct answer if he were aware that he would be punished with an electric shock each time he was wrong.* The Teacher and Learner would communicate with each other via a sound system.

The booth shared by the Experimenter and Teacher included a rheostat device measuring electric power in increments up to 450 volts, and a button. Each time the Learner gave a wrong answer, heard over the sound system, the Teacher was to press the button, giving the unseen Learner an electric shock. What's more, every wrong answer triggered a turn of the rheostat and a boost in the voltage delivered to the Learner.

Most of the Learners' answers were wrong, and their responses to the first few shocks were good-natured. But as the voltage increased, the responses grew more pained and frantic. Eventually the Learner began begging to be freed from the chair, crying out that the shocks were agonizing. Some, either before or during the experiment, declared that they were suffering from a heart ailment.

When Teachers began questioning the Experimenters, pointing out their concern for the Learner's survival, they were told that the experiment was to continue. If the Teacher balked, he was given a series of verbal prods, indicating that the procedure was an important step in measuring learning skills, and that the Teachers would not be held responsible for anything that went wrong. Even when there was no response from the Learner, the Teacher was ordered to raise the

* All participants were male—this was 1961, after all.

voltage and move on to the next question—all the way up to delivering a lethal 450 volts. At that point, it was agreed, the experiment would end.

In reality, of course, no electrical current was being sent to the Learner. None of the Teachers grasped this during the experiment. They were led to believe that powerful shocks were being delivered to the unfortunate Learner over and over again.

In all, forty Teachers participated in the series. Before things began, Milgram described the procedure and asked senior psychology students to guess how many Teachers would inflict the maximum voltage on the Learner, knowing that it could (and probably would) be lethal. The average guess was 1.2 percent. He posed the same question to forty psychiatrists, who predicted that fewer than 4 percent of Teachers would continue past the 300-volt level and barely one-tenth of 1 percent would actually administer the 450-volt shocks.

They were mistaken.

In the first set of experiments twenty-six of the forty volunteer Teachers went all the way to the end, pushing the button and believing they were sending 450 volts of electricity into the body of an unseen Learner who had not made a sound since the 300-volt shock had supposedly struck him. Many Teachers were uncomfortable about doing so. Many were sweating, shaking, groaning and laughing nervously. But they did what they were told and what, in their heart of hearts, they knew was morally wrong.

What does this have to do with business?

To me, it's clear that people whose morals we would judge to be as good as any other American's are capable of becoming agents in terrible, even horrific situations if their authority figure either assures them that they are doing the right thing or openly practices similar behavior. Even when they cannot avoid recognizing that their actions are incompatible with fundamental standards of behavior, few people have the moral strength to resist authority.

In the long-ago Yale experiment, authority wore a white coat and held a clipboard. In business, authority approves your salary, monitors your performance and decides if you have a future with the company. Today, the person who is the embodiment of power and authority in the United States of America wears a tailored suit, a bizarre hair style and resides in the White House.

My opposition to Donald Trump may sound like partisan politicking to some. Well, it's not. Since the day I first qualified to vote as a U.S. citizen, I have favored Republican candidates. I still do. Nonetheless, I respect those on the Democrat side who, I know, share as much love for this country and respect for its institutions as I do.

Whatever our party affiliation, those of us who oppose Trump, his actions and his policies understand that it is not enough to widely criticize the man and what he stands for. We need to be vocal about what concerns us, propose an antidote and take action that will not only reverse the damage he has done, but elevate the discourse and behavior in many areas of our society.

Let's begin with business.

STEP ONE: Start Seeing Business as a Community

Earlier, I characterized business as a community of sorts. Regardless of their product or service, or the location, size or competitive position of their company, most businesspeople share various values and goals. We gather at Rotary Club meetings and business development groups to share our views and concerns. We speak the same language of profit and loss, regulations and financing, markets and competitors, and from time to time, of course, of government actions good and bad. Whatever your political view, that's a community for sure. If you're a businessperson, at any level and in any capacity, you are a member of a community and *we are not immune to the influence of community members*. Keep that in mind.

We share the values that our communities share, especially those of the role models within our community. Sometimes this is conscious on several levels and in various ways. It's a natural human response. We are all social creatures, after all. If most of the people whose company we enjoy and whose values we admire play golf or attend concerts or support a specific charity, chances are we'll pick up a golf club or do whatever it takes to enable us to participate.

And at other times the actions of other community members—especially those with power and influence—give us permission to act in a manner that may not be our normal behavior. That's why we need to pay attention to the way our communities are shaped and the habits of character they encourage.

This is not just my opinion, by the way. And I'll admit it's not a new one. In fact, it's more than two thousand years old. The guy who first proposed it was Aristotle, the last of the great Greek philosophers. Challenge my views if you like, but good luck challenging his.

Aristotle had a thing about human virtues: he was in favor of them. He believed a moral virtue enabled humans to follow the main purpose of being human, which was to reason. Reason, he believed, is the quality that enables us to recognize and choose the middle ground between going too far and not going far enough in our actions, emotions and desires.*

Think about that. It's a simple but profound idea.

Our emotions may make us rage over some event or situation that we believe threatens us in some way. It's *reason* that prevents us from reacting with violence. We all have various desires as well. Our *reason* provides the control we need to either discard or satisfy those desires according to *community* values. Aristotle used this idea as the basis for his Golden Mean, the balance between two extremes. Courage may be an admirable quality, but too much of it without wisdom leads to recklessness and too little leads to cowardice.

You may dismiss this as a "middle of the road" approach—not an admirable position in some quarters these days. But as a standard for living a comfortable and productive life, and being tolerant of the opinions of others, is there any other measure? Aristotle did not preach theories or principles. He wasn't prepared to lay down hard and fast rules or even the kinds of admonitions our parents might

* This may be the first book to mention Donald Trump and Aristotle in the same thought process.

have aimed at us as children ("How would you like everyone to act the way you do?"). He did not believe in an absolute measure of "good" to guide our moral decisions, nor that there is a conflict between pursuing our self-interest and living comfortably within a community.

Rather, Aristotle proposed that our ability to reason would—or should—guide our ethical decisions, keeping them in line with, and relative to, the values espoused by the community with which we identify.

Almost 2,500 years later, Stanley Milgram proved that, if given approval by authority figures, either overtly or covertly, most of us will engage in behavior that we would normally avoid or scorn. Why? Because we tend to position our values and behavior according to those demonstrated by other people. This is proven every day, especially in large cities where the action of one person to stop a mugging on the street, object to racist or sexist comments on a subway or step forward to assist a disabled person prompts sudden support from bystanders. Most people will stand around, choosing not to become involved until someone else takes the action that everyone knows is necessary. They don't need advice to do it. They simply need an example as tacit permission. This is admirable when it produces a positive result, such as avoiding injury and despair to innocent victims. It is much less so when the modeling behavior succeeds in our rejection of doing the right thing. And, as Milgram's model confirms, our inclination to act in a manner that might otherwise conflict with our values becomes more powerful when modeled by an authority figure.

Donald Trump is not likely to advise every businessperson in America to find a way to avoid paying taxes (and conceal the fact), to declare corporate bankruptcy multiple times and leave creditors at a loss, to defend his or her views with outright lies and call them "alternative facts," or to implement any of the several other dubious strategies he has chosen to employ.

He doesn't have to. His position as president and commander in chief justifies those actions to many people. As the ultimate authority figure in America, he models behavior on a national scale—for better or for worse, knowingly or unwittingly. Each time he shifts the moral meter lower on the spectrum, countless numbers of people adjust their idea of permissible behavior as well. The result: his low standard of ethical (or unethical) behavior lowers the bar for an entire nation.

We like to think our personal ethics are fixed and immutable, but they are not always. Our ethical behavior is often inconsistent and at times hypocritical. We may feel justified in taking actions that are at odds with values we have held dear through much of our lives simply because we see others, particularly authority figures, modeling that less-than-principled behavior for us. In essence, we become blind to our values, and deaf to the voice of our conscience.

Leaders of all stripes in all sectors of life play many roles. Surely among their most important tasks are to inspire those who follow them and to set a standard of behavior for all. We should not—we *must* not—accept standards based on prejudice, greed, deceit and propaganda.

How Much Does It Cost to Maximize Profits? And Who Pays?

You probably know of situations in which someone—perhaps yourself—went against their better judgment because doing so had the approval of authority, or was an opportunity either to make a profit or avoid a loss. Sometimes, as occurred in the greatest disaster of America's space program, it was all three.

I remember the shock, in January 1986, of hearing that the Challenger space shuttle had exploded shortly after its launch in Florida. Watching the event repeated over and over on television news for the next several days was the most horrifying scene most of us in America had witnessed until the 9/11 attacks on the World Trade Center. The investigation that followed opened a window on the scene at NASA: engineers alarmed at the conditions of the launch, and their capitulation in the face of demands based on the pursuit of profit.

On the day before the launch, the weather forecast for the next morning was for clear skies but unseasonably cold temperatures. In fact, the thermometer was expected to drop to 18 degrees Fahrenheit overnight and remain below freezing at launch time the following morning. Engineers at Morton Thiokol*, the company that had built the Challenger's primary launch rocket, suggested that NASA delay the launch. The shuttle was designed to be launched at temperatures above 40°F. At lower temperatures, the engineers feared that some components would not operate as planned. They were particularly worried about the O-rings sealing the launch rocket's fuel cylinders together. The rings were classified a "Criticality 1" component. Under NASA's own rules, any condition threatening the performance of a component in that category should cause cancellation of a launch.[24]

The engineers at Thiokol, who were interested in hard facts and performance over profit and loss, spoke to NASA managers the night before the launch. Their message was simple and direct: Operating the shuttle at these low temperatures could lead to catastrophic failure of at least one critical component; delay the launch until at least later in the day when temperatures would rise to a safe level.

At first, Thiokol management supported the view of their engineers. When NASA objected, sometimes with outrage—one NASA manager shouted back at the engineers, "My God, Thiokol, when do you want me to launch—next April?"—Thiokol executives changed their minds, agreed with NASA, and approved the launch. Upon hearing this, one Thiokol engineer predicted that the Challenger would blow up.[25]

Why did the NASA managers insist on rejecting the warning from Thiokol engineers that it would be too risky to attempt a launch at such low temperatures? And why did the Thiokol engineers' bosses change their mind and refuse to support their own experts? In the case of Thiokol, the answer is simple and predictable: NASA was a client whose contract to Thiokol was worth hundreds of millions of dollars. A serious disagreement with NASA bigwigs could threaten the contract.

NASA's reasoning was a little convoluted. The Challenger launch was to send the first female astronaut into orbit, marking a major step forward in the space program. Moreover, that night President

* The company was formed as a result of a 1982 merger between Morton-Norwich and Thiokol Inc. The companies split in 1989; Thiokol now functions under the name Cordant Technologies.

Ronald Reagan was to deliver his State of the Union speech, in which he planned to mention the Challenger launch and praise it as representative of America's great achievements.

Were the joint decisions of Thiokol an abandonment of ethics or simply a miscalculation that can occur in many situations? Here's my answer: Hundreds of millions of dollars in potential earnings or losses were involved. The president's image and prestige were involved. And seven gifted and innocent individuals died as a direct result. How many dollars and how much prestige were their lives worth?

These people ignored their better judgment to shift their standards of what is good and right in the face of pressure, authority and circumstances. Let's remember that these were dedicated professionals associated with a prestigious program. We might assume that they would not be easily persuaded to take action that betrayed so much of their training and expertise. Yet they did. Lacking strong, explicit operating principles and values, their decision-making went off the rails, subverting what was right to satisfy immediate, short-term demands of the situation.

No Business Has an Absolute Right to Exist

That's an intentionally provocative statement to make an important point, perhaps one of the most important messages in the book. It may disturb some people, but in the total scheme of things it is true.

Corporations are not the product of a universal Creator. They are the product of people's ambitions, and their existence is formalized by governments that believe and trust (or ought to believe and trust) that the corporations exist to provide goods and services of benefit to the community as well as profits for the corporation. That's why governments grant certain benefits to corporations, such as limited liability and a sense of identity and existence beyond the people involved in them. The underlying assumption is that the actions of any given corporation enrich the community as well as the proprietors.

One more time: Every business, and those who participate in it, functions as part of a community and thus has an obligation to serve that community ethically. In the interests of pursuing and maximizing profit—a totally acceptable *raison d'être* for all businesses—decisions made in confidence have an impact on the very community companies are expected to serve and respect. That's fine. Except when the firm's respect for ethics takes a holiday.

Markets are very effective at many things, including establishing value and responding to improvements. Thanks to the confidential nature of business, however, they are not an effective means of preventing ethical missteps because corporations too often conceal them in the name of maintaining bottom-line profits, market share and competitive advantage. By the time ethical lapses become apparent, several years may have passed. The damage may be toxic waste pollution left behind by a company long out of business. Or it can be lives lost unnecessarily.

No self-respecting businessperson would claim or admit to intentionally polluting the environment or making business decisions that cost people their lives. That sort of irresponsible and devastating business behavior happens only when those who make these decisions have become deaf and blind to ethical standards in pursuit of profit.

Ethical blindness can take various forms. It can be indirect, such as cashing in on relationships with third parties, leaving offenders free to simultaneously pocket profits and wash their hands of guilt. This has occurred among giant pharmaceutical firms manufacturing drugs for rare diseases or treatments of unusual forms of cancer. The number of patients requiring these treatments may be a few thousand at any given time, and the cost of manufacturing the drugs required could be very low. Dramatically raising the price of the drug could give a boost to the firm's profits, but the move would risk damaging the company's valued reputation.

What to do? Easy. Sell the marketing rights of the drugs to a smaller, less known firm who can raise the price by a factor of five or ten times or more and easily absorb the bad press. The giant pharmaceutical firm keeps turning out the drugs, raises its wholesale price dramatically, boosts its bottom line and maintains its shining public face.*

* For details on an actual occurrence of this kind of behaviour, see Alex Berenson, "A Cancer Drug's Big Price Rise Is Cause for Concern," *New York Times*, March 12, 2006.

Another form is opportunity blindness, like the kind practiced when Sears sought to improve sales and profits from auto repairs by speeding up the performance of its mechanics. The company set an hourly goal of $147 in repairs and service for each mechanic; those whose work fell below that level were at risk of losing their jobs.

You can guess what happened, even if the Sears executives couldn't. Not taking time to do things correctly, the mechanics performed unsatisfactory work, overcharged for their services, and often made repairs and installed parts that were unnecessary.

The negative outcome of the Sears attempt to maximize profit was easily predictable by anyone with an objective point of view. It would also serve, you might think, as an object lesson for all service-based companies to avoid policies that practically invite employees to wander down unethical paths, on the lookout for fatter profits for their bosses and a few extra bucks for themselves.

Unfortunately, business leaders don't always learn from the mistakes and ethical missteps of others. Corporate executives often turn their back on both ethics and basic psychology when presented with such schemes. If reminded by others of the inherent drawbacks to the plan they tell themselves, "This time it's different."* But it never is.

Unhealthy Practices from a Health Provider

Like most people, I grew up assuming that the people who care for our health—doctors, nurses, therapists and so on—represent a special class of individuals. They sacrifice much, invest enormous amounts of time and money to qualify for their positions, and dedicate themselves to saving lives and relieving suffering. The vast majority do. But when opportunities to make outrageous profits appear, decency can take a fatal turn. As it did with HealthSouth Corporation a few years ago.

The company was one of the country's largest providers of healthcare services. At its height the publicly traded company operated in

* This phrase was labeled "The four most dangerous words in investment" by legendary investor Sir John Templeton.

every U.S. state plus Puerto Rico, Canada, Australia, the United Kingdom and Saudi Arabia, boasting $4.5 billion in annual revenue. But when the company's CEO conveniently sold $75 million of his shares in the company just a few days before the firm reported a major loss, it triggered (surprise!) a major investigation by the U.S. Securities and Exchange Commission.

The findings were astonishing. The company that had been dedicated to relieving pain for its patients had exerted major pain on its shareholders, thanks to false accounting over several years. The technique was simple: HealthSouth claimed imaginary profits—so imaginary and so extensive that the claims almost qualified as Trump-level B.S. In some years, the company's income was inflated as much as 4,700 percent beyond actual earnings.

The firm's CEO, Richard M. Scrushy, fought criminal and civil charges, eventually losing on both, and was sentenced to almost seven years in prison. Successfully sued by HealthSouth investors, he was ordered by the civil court to repay the company $2.8 billion. He served the prison sentence. It's unclear if he wrote a personal check to shareholders for the almost $3 billion.

How could things possibly go so wrong? Where was the oversight to prevent such a scam? Whatever the answers, the process of looking for them is essentially academic because if HealthSouth had identified and lived by clear corporate values, the fraud would never have happened.

When Human Lives Encounter the Bottom Line

The most common form of ethical blindness is directly motivated, and occurs in organizations that claim to be guided by acceptable ethical standards. And they usually are, until the bottom line is threatened. Then nothing—including human lives—stands in the way of covering the company's profits and, to put it bluntly, their own asses.

Remember the story of the Ford Explorer's flaws and the company's efforts to correct them at the lowest possible cost? This wasn't the first time that Ford had acted in such a manner. You might think it had learned its lesson with the Pinto almost twenty years earlier. Apparently, it hadn't.

Almost from the day the compact Pinto first appeared on U.S. highways, its defect became widely known and chillingly hazardous. The car grew notorious for bursting into flames in rear-end collisions and incinerating its occupants. The cause was a basic design flaw that the company had been alerted to by crash tests conducted just before its introduction. Ford executives decided to do nothing about it. Why? Because the company was geared to begin production, Volkswagen was stealing the sales of compact cars in America, and delaying the launch would cost the company millions.

Later, it was revealed that Ford executives did a cost-benefit analysis in line with every business school guideline. The analysis indicated that it would be cheaper to pay lawsuits emanating from collision damages than to halt production and make the repairs.[26] No one asked the estimated two dozen Pinto drivers and passengers who died in fiery crashes, or the dozens more who survived with horrific burns, how they felt about the memo.

It bears repeating: The purpose of business is to generate profit for its owners *and* deliver benefits of various kinds to the communities in which they operate.

There is no shortage of examples to confirm the credibility of this premise. They include the largest and smallest of firms. And they also, it should be noted, derive from single enlightened individuals. Like Bill Gates. He and his wife, Melinda, founded their charitable foundation in 1999 and its current endowment is $50 billion or more; their philanthropy undoubtedly helped to elevate the image of Bill and Melinda as well as that of Microsoft itself. Similarly, Paul Newman's pledge to donate all of his salad dressing company's profit to community- and health-related organizations generated an immediate sales boost that continues to resonate long after the founder's death.[27] These are oversized examples, to be sure. But countless other firms, under the leadership of people who operate according to values-based principles, are committed to demonstrating community responsibility as well as achieving commercial success in their operations.

There is, or should be, no conflict in those goals. But alas, there always is. From time to time we encounter a large, prestigious corporation whose gaze is totally inward and whose recognition of the rights of the community in which it operates is entirely erased. Even when that community includes the entire world.

5

Das Auto. Die Dummkopfs.

THE FORD EXPLORER, the Ford Pinto, and now Volkswagen. Am I unfairly fingering automotive companies when addressing unethical corporate conduct? I think not.

There are several good reasons for examining the behavior of car companies. First, because they are so critical to the economy of every industrialized country in the world. Despite the size and success of Apple, Samsung and similar firms, automotive companies still make a big impact on us economically. Also, next to a home, buying a new car represents the largest single consumer purchase most of us will make—and we may do it several times. Poor automobile quality makes more than an impact on our bank accounts; it can cost lives as well, including our own. Finally, car companies just seem to find new ways of getting things wrong in the way they make their vehicles and the way they seem to avoid ethical behavior. Like, of course, Volkswagen.

The basic facts are well-known. In its effort to have its diesel-powered vehicles achieve air quality standards, the company programmed the cars to modify the engine performance during emissions testing. The cars reached the standards during the tests. On the road, the exhaust gases were exceptionally dirty, but the performance of the cars matched the company's claim to drivers. They had a good guy/bad guy personality. In the labs they were good guys, managing to run traditionally "dirty" diesel engines cleanly. On the road, however, they were bad guys, although still satisfying the expectations of owners with good gas mileage and all-round impressive performance.

So they were cheaters. But there's more to it than that. Volkswagen management outright lied for an entire year after news of the scandal broke. The difference in emissions levels between testing and on-the-road real-world performance was the result of a "technical glitch," they said. When confronted with proof that the cars employed a "defeat device," management made things worse by initially blaming their engineers—the very people within the company who had been responsible for VW's vaunted quality reputation over the years. Everyone quickly grasped that the engineers were being made scapegoats, and the realization added another layer of smelly mud over the entire company. This wasn't some kind of corporate misdemeanor, a bunch of the gang getting together over lager and schnapps to play a prank on some stiff-necked white-coated inspectors. This was major chicanery on a global scale. And a betrayal of their own employees.

News of VW's fraudulent behavior stunned many people who believed the company represented an ethical entity in comparison with the rest of the automobile industry. As things turned out, VW was just as "dirty" as everyone else where efforts to reduce the environmental impact of cars and trucks were concerned. It's not a recent development. Auto companies have found ways to dupe the system for decades.

Think You Know Who the Bad Guys Are? You Don't.

Here's a partial list of the many ways auto manufacturers have cheated and lied about their products to satisfy regulators and earn approval from consumers—all in the name of boosting their bottom lines:

- In 1973 Chrysler, Ford, GM and Toyota were ordered to remove ambient temperature switches that enriched the fuel mixture during warm-up periods, raising emissions well above agreed-upon levels. The companies had first denied the switches existed.
- In 1996 GM paid a then-record fine of $11 million and recalled almost half a million vehicles when caught using a similar technique to VW's to alter the emissions levels of their cars. The levels of carbon monoxide (CO) and unburned hydrocarbons (UHCs) were significantly higher than claimed; both are a major component of smog and a contributor to poor air quality.
- Ford was caught cheating in a similar manner when sixty thousand 1997 Econoline vans were discovered to have devices that cut emissions during testing and restored them for normal use.
- Seven heavy truck engine manufacturers—Caterpillar, Cummins, Detroit Diesel, Mack Trucks, Navistar, Renault and Volvo—paid the largest fine to date ($83.4 million) for cheating on emissions testing.

Whatever your views on the Environmental Protection Agency and their mandate to reduce emissions from motor vehicles on American roads, the law requiring companies to meet standards was on the books through all of these escapades. Some companies met the requirements of the law, assuming that paying the price of compliance was the only way to meet the standards ethically. To the others, meeting the prescribed benchmarks seemed to be a fine idea as long as it didn't entail extra engineering efforts and cause a blip on their bottom line. To those others, short-term profits were far more important than principles. Most observers agree that the VW incident was uniquely outrageous. VW, one industry safety expert noted, "took it to another level of sophisticated deception we've never seen before."

The entire VW scandal was a matter of ethics versus profit. No other definition is necessary. And while it's logical to assume that the degree of fraud that occurred at VW must have had at least the knowledge and encouragement of top executives, there was plenty of incentive to maintain the ruse. Manipulating the vehicles' software gave many levels and divisions of the company a boost. Marketing and advertising could assure environmentalists that, contrary to expectations, the VW diesels did not kick out more pollutants than gasoline-powered vehicles. This wasn't just an incentive to purchase a VW diesel; it was confirmation of VW's advanced engineering expertise, and an enhancement of the company's overall engineering standards and concern for the environment. Not anymore, of course.*

This scandal also followed the law of unintended consequences. Because of the blatant lie spun globally by VW for almost a year, other suspicions were raised. If VW could so blatantly deceive the world about emissions from its diesel vehicles, what else might it be lying about? Soon governments everywhere began putting the company under bright lights in a closed room and demanding answers. Australia looked into possible violations of consumer and safety standards; Germany dug into the personal background of the VW CEO; Italian police raided VW offices in Bologna; the Netherlands began demanding millions of dollars back for VW cars purchased by the government on the basis of bogus emissions levels; Norway's sovereign wealth fund—one of the largest investors in VW—launched a class-action lawsuit; Switzerland banned sales of all VW diesel vehicles; and on and on. In total, more than twenty countries bombarded the company with lawsuits and restrictions.[28]

So how much did all of this cost VW?

In absolute dollars, the amount is breathtaking. At the peak of the scandal the renowned bank Credit Suisse added up all the fines, penalties, secondary costs and something called "negative knock-on effects." Then they hung the price tag on the mess: as much as US$86 billion.[29] For a bit of perspective, this would eclipse the cost of the biggest industrial disaster to that point: US$53.8 billion for BP's 2010 Deepwater Horizon oil spill in the Gulf of Mexico.

In terms of lost reputation, the price may be incalculable. It will take years of the company toeing the line and the development of new car models that excite the buying public to even begin restoring trust in the brand.

* The scandal also affected Audi, a leading luxury car brand.

Bad Guys Don't Just Make Cars; Some Make Drugs

No one can question the importance of assessing ethical behavior on the part of automotive companies. How, for example, can you possibly ignore the ethics of an organization that decides it's more economical to pay for deaths and injuries resulting from defects in their products than to take measures to prevent or at least reduce the incidence in the first place?

But the auto industry is hardly the only sector that appears ready to waive morals and principles where maximizing profit is concerned. In fact, some people may consider automakers pikers when compared with pharmaceutical companies.

The people who research, test, manufacture and supply life-saving drugs do a wonderful service to humanity. And many of them have grown enormously wealthy and powerful as a result. In that view both the companies and society as a whole have benefited.

I'm not interested in accusing any corporation or any individual for achieving wealth as a direct result of business success. I couldn't claim to be an ardent capitalist if I did. Only when the pursuit of wealth shoves aside any semblance of moral responsibility do I view it as destructive to our values and needs as a society.

Some recent examples have scored record highs—or lows—on the scale of outrageous behavior. They include the infamous decision made by the CEO of Turing Pharmaceuticals within days of acquiring rights to the drug Daraprim. The drug, used to treat those suffering from toxoplasmosis, a life-threatening parasitic infection, had been priced at $13.50 per tablet. Without either warning or necessity, Turing CEO Martin Shkreli raised the price to $750. Was this legal? Of course. Nothing on the books restricts a company from setting any price the market can bear. Was it ethical? You know the answer.*

* When the outrage against Shkreli and his company's move grew loud and wide enough for Congress to launch an inquiry, Shkreli stepped down as CEO, just in time to face a government indictment charging him with participating in fraudulent activities related to hedge funds he had founded. (Department of Justice, U.S. Attorney's Office, Eastern District of New York, "Former Hedge Fund Manager and New York Attorney Indicted in Multimillion Dollar Fraud Scheme." December 17, 2015.)

How to Make Excess Profits and Pass the Blame

Just as Americans were getting over the actions of Turing and its CEO, word broke about a similar price-jacking scheme in the industry. This time it involved the drug company Mylan, marketers of EpiPen. If you have a child or know of one who may suffer a potentially fatal anaphylactic shock from allergic reactions to foods (1 in 13 American children face this risk[30]), you know about EpiPen. The device administers the antidote epinephrine, and most children diagnosed with the risk carry one at all times. While other treatments exist, the EpiPen has long been considered the industry standard. EpiPen is as identifiable to people suffering risk of a serious allergic reaction as Kleenex is to people in need of a facial tissue. The market for EpiPen and similar devices is sized at about $1.5 billion annually.

Mylan does not manufacture EpiPens; they're made by a division of Pfizer. In September 2016 an engineering consultancy estimated that it cost Pfizer about $10 to manufacture and package a two-pack of EpiPens. The cost of the actual drug within each EpiPen was about $1.

When Mylan acquired the rights to market EpiPens in 2007, the price of a two-pack was $100. I'll do the math for you: That's a 1,000-percent mark-up on basic costs. Could Mylan and Pfizer make a decent profit from such a margin? You would think so. But in 2016, Myland kicked the retail price to $600 per two-pack, or $300 for an item with a laid-down cost of $10. Or maybe $15, just to account for any increase in manufacturing cost. Apparently a 1,000 percent mark-up was not sufficient.

Not in the United States, at least. The same two-pack north of the border in Canada was priced at about one-third of the price that U.S. families and insurance providers were charged, and even less in Great Britain. Why the difference? Among the various reasons: both countries have national health care systems that engage in tough price negotiations before a medical product can be listed for coverage by them. The primary reason for the U.S. price is the basic capitalist guideline about charging whatever the market will bear.

This takes us back to an earlier question about the freedom to earn a profit from business activities versus benefiting the community in which a company functions. Can social good take precedence over profit? To some (including, I suspect, Donald Trump), the question may sound like a far-left-wing battle cry, a call to action against the basis of American free enterprise. So I'll rephrase it: Should pharmaceutical firms and related companies be held to a higher standard than other industries?

The answer lies neither in left-wing nor right-wing points of view. It lies instead in a basic question of economics: How can maximizing profit be the sole objective of a company if the same goal prevents a consumer from purchasing their life-saving (or at least curative) product? For any company, no matter what industry they are in, that's a management decision based on a variety of factors including product life, competitive activity, distribution channels and others. But the ethical issues around the economics become cloudy when the product—in this case EpiPen—is effective at saving lives.

Where many industries are concerned, consumers will vote with their wallets and choose not to participate if the demand drops beneath the market price. That's fine when the demand is elastic and the decision to buy is discretional. Need proof? Try selling Christmas ornaments in January or snow shovels in July. But what choice do parents of a young child have if the child may suffer a potentially fatal reaction to something as common and unpredictable as a single peanut in a cookie? Do we concede that pharmaceutical suppliers can put a price on human life? And that they can set that price at whatever maximizes their bottom line—which often means boosting performance bonuses for top executives?

No one said setting and maintaining ethical standards would be easy. But it is essential. We cannot expect to run our businesses with the same disregard for principles displayed by the current chief executive of the United States and not have our society become like the Wild West. Corporate values are a key element in creating and sustaining a balance in society between free enterprise and the social good. Economics involves much more than jacking the corporate profit report to make shareholders happy and executives rich; it's a *social science* that takes into account the interplay of every aspect of society, and how the relationships between individuals, businesses and government, among others, affect and influence one another.

So no matter what the company or what the industry, shouldn't every business be as concerned about the impact of its practices and principles on all its stakeholders at the same time it strives to improve its own economics?

6

Did We Not Get the Enron Memo?

ALMOST TWENTY YEARS ago, the collapse of Enron destroyed the myth that some businesses are too big and too wealthy to fail. All these years later, it's still a textbook example of a corporation defying virtually every legal and ethical guideline to enrich its top executives. Even today, the size of the catastrophe makes it sound like an outline by a Hollywood scriptwriter pitching a disaster movie to a skeptical producer: *Investors in the company lose $60 billion virtually overnight. Enron partners and suppliers lose an equal amount of money. Much of the loss represents funding for the investors' retirement. More than twenty thousand Enron employees lose their jobs and $2 billion in their pension savings.*

The scope of the collapse and the shockwaves it spread throughout America and globally makes any reference to Enron in a book on business ethics almost unnecessary. Enron stands as more than a sad milestone in the history of American business. When discussing unethical business practices and portraying a victory for greed over decency, it has become a cliché. But remember: A cliché is a cliché *because it is true.*

To refresh our collective memories:

Enron was founded in 1985 via a merger between two relatively small Texas energy companies. Within fifteen years the firm claimed annual revenues of more than $100 billion, confirmed by Arthur Andersen, the company's highly regarded auditor. Enron's status and performance were so impressive that for six consecutive years it was labeled "America's Most Innovative Company" by *Fortune* magazine.

If performance awards and the assurance of one of the country's most respected auditing companies wasn't enough, anyone doubting Enron's enormous business success could turn to the company's *Code of Ethics* booklet, which began:

> As officers and employees of Enron Corporation, its subsidiaries and its affiliated companies, we are responsible for conducting the business affairs of the companies in accordance with all applicable laws and in a moral and honest manner.

That's simple and direct. But the code of ethics goes on for another sixty-plus pages: thousands of words of boilerplate text and empty promises. The first lesson to be learned from Enron may well be that a company's dedication to ethical behavior is in inverse proportion to the number of words it takes to say, "We promise to be good boys and girls!"

The *Code of Ethics* did not prevent Enron's top executives from behaving like children in a candy store. The investigations following its collapse in late 2001 revealed a bewildering blend of institutionalized, systematic and creative accounting fraud. The creative aspect was realized through special-purpose entities (SPEs) located offshore and thus out of sight of probing eyes. The fictitious SPEs were employed, Enron claimed, as a form of hedging to protect Enron's asset base. Enron executives established several SPEs, transferring massive blocks of stock to them in return for cash, which appeared on the company's balance sheet. In effect, Enron issued IOUs from its own fictional subsidiaries and claimed the IOUs as equivalent to cash assets.

This was merely one way the company fooled everyone who didn't occupy an office in the top floor executive suite. Others—employees, auditors, bankers and essentially the rest of the world—believed what they were being told. When the company began losing money, the executives would launch another bucket of SPEs or apply some other device and turn a concrete loss into a mythical profit. Soon they were in a death spiral that they couldn't stop. Or maybe they didn't want it to stop, because with every declared new profit level, the Enron stock price rose like a thermometer in Death Valley in July.

It was all too much to resist. The executive group began selling their Enron shares at ever-increasing prices. They spread the word to family and friends, who bought and sold shares, pocketing hundreds of millions of dollars in profit.

When things unraveled and the scope of the fraud became known, many people were belted with two conflicting emotions. One was shock at the amount of money being tucked away by the executives who perpetrated the scheme and the *chutzpah* it took to maintain the facade when it was obvious that the entire scam was collapsing around them. The other was surely envy. There are several ways to make an obscenely large amount of money, all of them dependent on very hard work and very good luck. The Enron gang had found a new way to pull it off with creative thinking, trusted confederates and a near-total lack of scruples.

The Garbage Has Been Picked Up, but the Smell Remains

Looking back at Enron, a fiasco to most but a tragedy to trusting investors and employees who saw years of their savings vanish, many people consider justice was done and future swindles prevented. They point to the harsh jail terms handed out—CEO Jeffrey Skilling received a 24-year prison sentence, later reduced to 14 years—and the creation of the *Sarbanes-Oxley Act*, which launched the biggest change in American securities law since the Great Depression.

All true. But in my book the biggest impact was not who went to jail or who lost their savings, or how the government reacted. It was the influence of Enron on the business world. Years later, for example, some other corporate leaders may even have used the Enron example to justify the steps they took—unprincipled actions that rocked financial foundations globally and inspired the Great Recession of 2008–09.

Their thinking likely went like this: *Skilling and others at Enron went to prison? Gee, that's too bad. If they had been more careful... if they had avoided the kinds of things that we know caused their downfall... they would have succeeded in keeping all that money. But we can do it right. All we need to do is keep our eye on the money and forget everything else, like ethics. After all, who ever paid for a Ferrari with ethics?* Or something like that.

A linkage exists between leaders who reject business ethics on a grand scale in pursuit of enormous wealth, and those who follow them: they generally choose a similar unscrupulous path to achieve personal, professional and corporate goals. Dozens of studies, both academic and empirical, confirm the effect that unprincipled leaders and role models have on those they employ and those they were elected to govern. Academics call it "parallel deviance,"[31] meaning that employees (and presumably citizens generally, to some degree) can be prone to imitating unethical conduct when they witness their leaders being rewarded for similar behavior.

Kenneth Lay, the chairman/CEO who led Enron to its dramatic and damaging implosion, had been celebrated in the business press for several years before things hit the fan. Hailed throughout the business world as an exceptional leader and brilliant strategist, Lay and his team kept defying conventional wisdom by constantly surpassing Wall Street's financial expectations. They weren't just successful executives running an over-achieving corporation while pocketing enormous financial rewards for their efforts, they were lauded as great heroes of American free enterprise and praised by people who either didn't care how they kept achieving the near impossible or chose not to look deep enough to discover it.

America loves heroes. Heroes represent much of what the country is about: doing good, abiding by the law, pursuing dreams, maintaining moral standards and treating others with respect. Until the bitter end, made especially bitter for the twenty thousand Enron employees and countless investors who trusted the management group, Enron served as a model for all that can be achieved through vision, acumen and hard work.

Nobody mentioned ethics.

The Enron catastrophe was soon joined by similar calamities involving WorldCom, Tyco and others—all once-thriving corporations plunged into ruin by the greed and immorality of their top executives. Many of the CEOs at these firms appeared to have invested more effort at financial engineering—searching for new ways to manipulate facts and figures to conceal unscrupulous actions—than at building their company by offering superior service and products.

Here's the real lesson worth pondering: Even with tighter regulations imposed on business through vehicles such as the *Sarbanes-Oxley Act*, nothing about the decisions made in Enron's boardroom and executive suite was so unique that it could not occur again in another company in another location at another time. In fact, it began happening all over again around the time that Lay, Skilling and other Enron fraudsters were indicted for their crimes.

Those Enron executives had no qualms about selling shares that they knew were backed by hollow facts and nonexistent assets. They had discovered a way to keep Enron's debt off its balance sheet. They took it further by encouraging Enron employees to invest their money, including their 401(k) plans, in Enron stock when they knew the share price was tumbling toward worthlessness, all while pocketing sky-high profits for themselves. And yes, some of the soon-to-be-worthless shares bought by the trusting employees had been the executives' own—made available when they sold them off for their own gain.

What does it take for highfliers like Skilling and the others to treat ordinary people with such scorn? Start with ego. Add unlimited arrogance and unfettered greed and watch the contempt for outsiders spread throughout the organization, thanks to parallel deviance. Because it did. Some of this disdain was captured on tape in a discussion between Enron middle managers, who sneered at the attitude of Californians and laughed at the amount of income Enron was pocketing via blatant manipulation of the power being supplied to customers.*

The same attitude prevailed when Wall Street firms Lehman Brothers, Bear Stearns, Goldman Sachs and others packaged worthless home mortgages into impressive and "secure" financial instruments, and peddled them around the world. Those who believed that Enron marked a demoralizing milestone for American business ethics discovered later that, compared with the Great Recession of 2008–09, Enron was like a bunch of rampant teenagers. Different conductors may have orchestrated the events, but they all played the same tune that sang of gluttony and malice.

The unifying message concerns the role of the leaders in each case. None of these schemes was initiated by middle managers. Each originated within the CEO's bailiwick, which set the tone that the behavior was more than acceptable—it was beneficial to the entire organization and thus to the individuals who supported it, ethics be damned. Mass abandonment of the principles that most, if not all, of the participants would claim to share made the schemes not only possible but, at the outset, enormously successful.

Three Kinds of Detours Off the Ethical Path

"Not everyone chose to follow the lead of Enron in search of wealth," you may suggest. Perhaps. But it doesn't take many to influence others directly and indirectly. Just six Enron executives were convicted

* In the now infamous Grandma Millie exchange recorded on November 30, 2000, two traders, identified as Kevin and Bob, discuss demands by California officials that Enron pay refunds to customers for the company's price-gouging actions:

KEVIN: *So the rumor's true? They're* [expletive] *takin' all the money back from you guys? All those* [sic] *money you guys stole from those poor grandmothers in California?*

BOB: *Yeah, Grandma Millie, man. But she's the one who couldn't figure out how to* [expletive] *vote on the butterfly ballot* [referring to the 2000 presidential election].

KEVIN: *Yeah, and now she wants her* [expletive] *money back for all the power you've charged for* [expletive] *$250 a megawatt hour.*

(Laughter)

of wrong-doing (a total of twenty people, including three British businessmen, were found guilty). It's not the number—it's their influence that's critical.

When it comes to wandering off the ethical path, psychologists categorize people in three broad levels: preconventional, conventional and principled.[32]

Preconventional subjects represent the lowest level. Their goal is to avoid punishment for their actions and look for partners in any unethical conduct, a one-hand-washes-the-other form of reciprocity.

Principled individuals occupy the highest level. They reflect on difficult decisions by assessing them according to their personal moral values, using any conflict with them as justification to walk away. They are—not surprisingly—least likely to engage in behavior that involves cheating, stealing, lying or defying community values.

Decades of research confirm that the majority of people fall into the middle conventional category. When faced with a decision that may involve dubious behavior, they look outside themselves for guidance by examining the behavior of others, including friends, family, coworkers and especially leaders.

Leaders make key decisions for all of us. In business, they determine the rewards and punishment imposed on employees. If the CEO of a large international company announces that the firm will pass up the chance to do business in a corrupt foreign nation because it would expose the company to the possibility of engaging in bribery and other unethical acts, it's a powerful principled message to everyone. And when the top executives of another company consistently bend rules as a means of acquiring business or boosting profits or sidestepping regulations, everyone understands that they will be forgiven for repeating the same actions in pursuit of the same objectives.

We all reason our way through ethical dilemmas. It's simply a matter of deciding what is the right thing to do and what is the wrong thing to do. Part of that reasoning involves the dark side of modeling theory, the one where we see others acting in a way that challenges our moral guidelines but promises benefits that are worth the risk of being caught or the guilt of breaking with our own standards.

Perhaps we can give Aristotle the last word on this part of the story:

> Men do wrong when they think it can be done and when they think it can be done by them; when they think that their action will either be undiscovered, or if discovered will remain unpunished; or, if it is punished, that the punishment will be less than the profit to themselves or to those for whom they care.[33]

Deeds, Not Words (1)

Whenever I hear a businessperson scoff at the importance of maintaining business ethics, suggesting that everything is based on maximizing profit, I want to ask them how ethical they are in their private life. "Do you lie to your children about your personal behavior? Do you cheat on your spouse, steal candy bars from the supermarket, write a fewer number of strokes than you took on your golf game card, take silverware home from dinner at a friend's home?" I would ask them. Most would be insulted and angry with me for asking those questions. But my queries would be fully justified.

Making a success of our personal lives is just as important as making a success of our business. Maybe even more important. You cannot guide one side of your life by following society's expectations, and guide the other side according to the law of the jungle. Not without a serious case of schizophrenia. One must dominate, and the side you choose for either role—personal or professional—will define your character, your leadership style and ultimately your success.

Excuses will be made, of course. They always are. Whether you are an entrepreneur determined to pull yourself to success by your bootstraps or a business professional scurrying your way up the corporate ladder with your eye on the summit, part of your motive will be profit—profit for you and profit for the business. Well, good luck to you. I've climbed that ladder and yanked on my bootstraps. I understand and applaud your goals. But while you're building the value of your net worth, give thought to the value of your reputation. Then ask yourself what is more important in the long run.

I have an idea for a poll I'd like to conduct someday. I would ask Americans from all walks of life to list the five historical figures, living or dead, whom they most admire. I would expect to hear of athletes, artists, religious leaders, philosophers and the entire gamut of achievers, including a few politicians perhaps. Then I would ask the qualities of these people that made them objects of such high esteem. The answers would range from personal character and generosity to technical achievements and courage. Few responses, I am sure, would be a version of "They made themselves very, very wealthy"!

Some may remain convinced that the only purpose in launching a business or throwing yourself into a corporate sprint is to garner obscene amounts of money, and do whatever it takes to accumulate it. Setting and maintaining a strict code of ethics, they may suggest, is a bunch of idealistic malarkey. So I would introduce them to Maxwell F. Anderson or read them the story of his poll at Harvard Business School (HBS). Anderson, an HBS student, had this wacky idea that Harvard MBA students should take an oath swearing they would act ethically as businesspeople after earning their degree and immersing themselves in business.

Harvard MBA students represent a highly competent and highly committed group of present or future business professionals whose career goals are at least as elevated as anyone with CEO ambitions. With all that motivation and training, how many would be concerned about something as trivial as vowing to act according to high ethical standards? Anderson was told by an HBS professor that fewer than one hundred students were likely to make the promise. Within a week he had gathered almost 350 pledges, and many more followed.[34]

Anderson's simple poll does not ensure, I agree, that every Harvard MBA graduate left the school with an undying conviction to set flawless standards for ethical behavior. But vowing to back words with deeds represents something of substance. Those of us who chose to be married in a public ceremony to make promises to our partner understand this. Breaking any vow we render in that manner is wrong and regrettable. I believe in the power of vows and the intent that they are made to be permanent. In a marriage, they represent personal and social responsibility—the promise to behave in a manner that meets the expectations of the person we are wedding and of the society we identify with. Having made the vow in the presence of others, we must prepare to be judged by our partner and by others.

Ethics Don't Cost. They Pay.

I propose that companies similarly think of business ethics as a means of meeting corporate social responsibility. Articulating shared corporate values and striving to adhere to them consistently makes an important pledge to employees, leaders, customers and other stakeholders about how you will conduct yourself as a business in relation to that entire community.

All of this ties into my point that maintaining high ethics in business is not a moralistic goal dictated by scripture, law, regulations or some other external source. Nor is principled corporate behavior simply the right thing to do. It's a practical concept. Forget the feel-good aspect, as valuable as it may be to us individually. Ethical behavior in business pays off, and I can prove it.

In the first two decades of the twentieth century, more than 2 million children aged ten to fourteen were employed full-time in America. They weren't hawking newspapers or sweeping floors. They worked in coalmines, bent on hands and knees to crawl along narrow cuts in the coal veins. They were favored by glassmakers to work alongside blazing furnaces set at 3,000 degrees Fahrenheit because, it was believed, young boys could tolerate intense heat better than adults. They toiled in canneries and textile mills, farms and factories, usually sixteen hours a day, growing up without a childhood and

THE PYRAMID OF SOCIAL RESPONSIBILITY[35]

Expectations of social responsibility should be no less applied to corporations than to individuals. Indeed, a strong case can be made that corporations have a much larger role to play, beyond their relative size as measured in assets and employees, than citizens. Most corporations recognize this not merely as an obligation but as a means of enhancing their public image, general influence and overall success.

The responsibilities were classified several years ago and assigned within four levels, beginning with Economic Responsibilities. Success at each level justifies assuming responsibilities in fulfilling the organization's role at the next higher level.

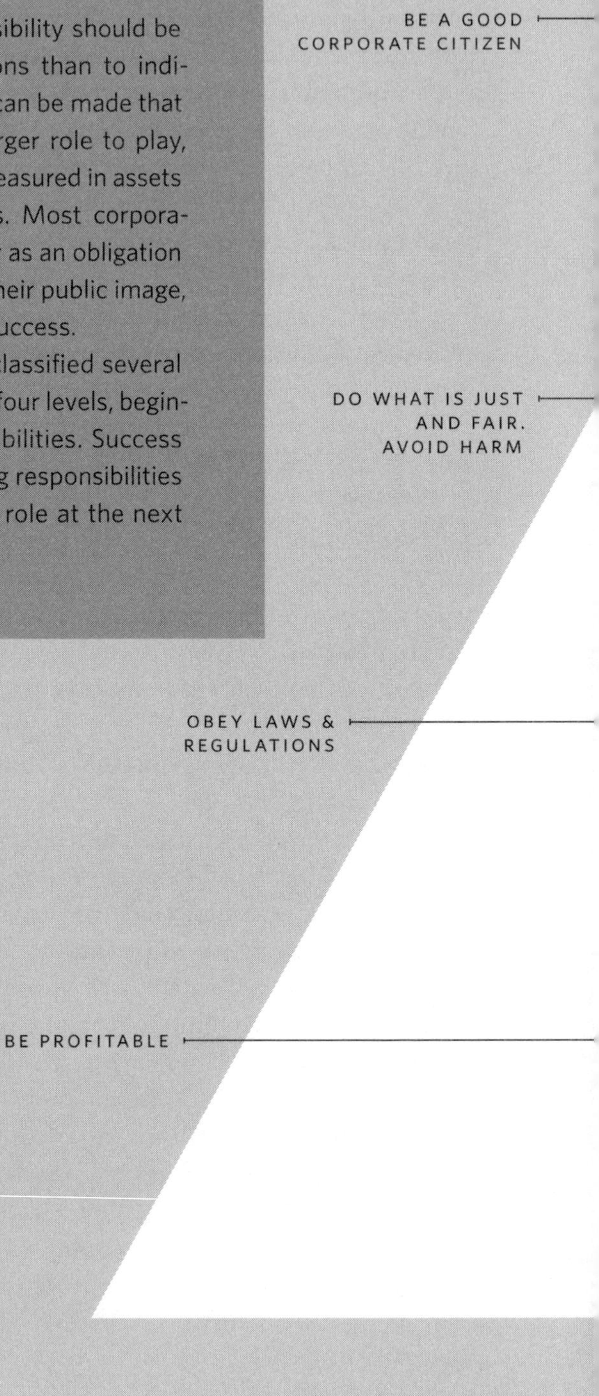

DESIRED BY SOCIETY

4 PHILANTHROPIC RESPONSIBILITIES

The peak of the Responsibility Pyramid encompasses *Philanthropic Responsibilities.* When both the basic responsibilities—Economic and Legal—are being met, and Ethical Responsibilities are being followed, consideration should be given to a firm's Philanthropic Responsibilities. This is often labeled "giving back to the community," which can sound as though the money had been stolen. I prefer to think of it as benefiting society with a share of the money available. Donating to community projects, helping charities, aiding the environment—they all represent a means of saying, "We identify with this community, and we want to see it develop and become enriched." Without being cynical about the motive for the decision, a company that fulfills its Philanthropic Responsibilities will see its image improve dramatically, leading to a rise in customer loyalty, aiding in attracting top-flight employees, and even a general improvement in bottom-line performance.

EXPECTED BY SOCIETY

3 ETHICAL RESPONSIBILITIES

With Economic and Legal Responsibilities accounted for, we encounter *Ethical Responsibilities*—moral guidelines that companies identify and sometimes express to reflect the standards of their owners, leaders and employees. These tenets are not imposed on the firm from the outside; they are agreed-upon, heeded and obeyed because they represent the character of the firm and those working within it. A firm's operating principles are often articulated in mission and vision statements, company codes of ethics or other tangible expressions of a company's shared values. They may be included in the organization's pledge to pay fair wages, avoid doing business with oppressive countries, establish environmentally friendly policies and so on.

REQUIRED BY SOCIETY

2 LEGAL RESPONSIBILITIES

After Economic Responsibilities come *Legal Responsibilities*, the need to work within the laws that apply to an organization generally and specifically. These can range from securities and commercial restrictions to labor and environmental regulations. Criminal law, of course, is a given. As much as we may find some aspects of legal compliance tedious, the responsibility for a corporation to obey the laws that apply to it must be acknowledged. No one can, or should try to, suggest that businesses operate free of legal obligations. Nor should we try to pick and choose the ones we want to obey. If following the law appears too arduous, our task should be to find a way to change the law, not ignore it.

REQUIRED BY SOCIETY

1 ECONOMIC RESPONSIBILITIES

In a corporate pyramid structure, the foundation of social responsibility is *Economic.* Companies, after all, must primarily be concerned with making a profit. Neither I nor anyone else should question the right of a corporation to earn profits for its owners and provide income for its employees. If a company cannot meet its economic responsibilities it has no reason, either moral or practical, to be in business.

rarely learning to read or write or acquire any skills and experiences beyond basic labor.[36]

What changed things? How were children eventually protected from such exploitation (including physical and sexual abuse in many cases) while forbidden from enjoying childhood, acquiring education, and helping to build a prosperous nation? Like the abolition of slavery, banning childhood labor was not purely an economic decision. It was the result of individuals and companies insisting on ethical standards that opposed such treatment. The assertion that children be permitted and encouraged not only to enjoy their lives but to acquire an education coincided with the enrichment of America, no matter how you choose to measure it. Higher standards of education spread across a broader cross-section of citizens made the country more efficient, more effective, more aspiring and, ultimately, wealthier. The move granted America the ability and ambition needed to build its economic and political prominence through the twentieth century. And it was achieved at least in part by raising ethical standards.*

No Excuses Permitted

Setting and maintaining standards of ethical behavior, as I acknowledged earlier, has grown complex for many corporate leaders. Like many decisions in business, the picture is rarely black and white. Too often it is viewed in shades of gray. But setting ethical guidelines and boundaries is simple and uncomplicated. Or should be.

When no obviously correct solution is available to a problem, good managers prioritize. Ethical decisions can be made in the same manner, eliminating the challenge of grappling with an otherwise ambiguous situation. Choosing whether to deal with a company, or

* Well into the twenty-first century, child labor remains prevalent in several countries around the globe, and its malfunction as an economic policy matches its failure to meet basic ethical standards. In three African nations—Guinea-Bissau, Mali and Ethiopia—more than half of children under the age of fourteen are engaged in full-time labor. All three countries are among the poorest in the world.

in a country, that pursues corrupt practices means setting priorities, establishing guidelines based on the priorities, and enforcing the guidelines without exception.

No Solomon-level wisdom is needed in many cases. If your company has international operations, it needs to set a policy of refusing to engage in bribery to secure business there. "But other guys are doing it!" is no excuse. American companies are forbidden to pay bribes to secure business, end of story. Still, the temptation remains. One solution is for members of an industry to connect with their peers and competitors—the "other guys"—and agree on a systematic way of shutting down the practice.

This may not be as difficult as it sounds. Bribery gives an unfair advantage to one firm over another because the bribe does not reflect the quality of the product or service being sold. If you or your company strive to achieve profits and success by outperforming your competition in various ways, bribery on their part destroys that distinction and makes such effort useless. Where does your hard work get you if the other guys just write a bigger check?

There's another downside. If knowledge of your company engaging in bribery becomes public, it can have a severely negative impact on domestic markets, slashing public trust in companies that engage in the practice. (Let's remember how quickly facts and opinions can blanket markets and nations via social media.) An industry that recognizes this and follows a policy of avoiding bribes can escape negative public reaction.

I sense that, in reaction to the bizarre rhetoric, irrational behavior and deficient ethics of Donald Trump, a demand for higher business ethics and greater social responsibility is about to emerge in American society. Some of it will arrive from other countries that are making great headway in reducing energy consumption, attaining maximum use of nonrenewable resources and introducing guidelines to cut unfairness and tension in the workplace. We may ignore them for a time, but we cannot resist these positive influences forever.

No one—especially no businessperson—is prepared to admit that his or her company engages in unethical behavior. There are many excuses for taking shortcuts where scruples are involved, and all are both flimsy and unacceptable. They range from "We were bending the rules a little" (read: *We did whatever we could get away with*) and "We were only following industry policy" (read: *Everybody else was doing it*) to "We were unaware of the restrictions against that practice" (read: *We looked the other way and pocketed the money*).

Excuses like these may save face, but they destroy trust. Trust is the lubricant that helps business run smoothly. Without trust, business loses the opportunity to function as a collaborative enterprise, which is what business is really all about. Or should be. A loss of trust comes at a price measured by the substantial legal fees we pay to ensure that companies do what we would expect them to do if they had high ethics and we had their trust.

Do the Right Thing

I have often speculated about a corporate policy that would reward executives not just according to their success at generating profit but for their achievement at maintaining and elevating the firm's ethical standards, energy consumption and resource sustainability. By aligning executive compensation with bottom-line performance exclusively, the signal sent to employees, shareholders, customers and the community as a whole is clear: the firm is concerned only with maximizing profits, and factors like ethical expectations and social performance don't matter worth a damn. If they did, their success would be reflected in executive-level compensation.

Making everyone in an organization accountable for ethical behavior, including the leaders—perhaps especially the leaders—all adds up to the concept of corporate citizenship, a role that all successful companies in America should practice to the extent of their capabilities.

At first glance, the goal of corporate citizenship sounds impractical and contradictory. Good corporate citizens are expected to generate higher standards of living and quality of life for the communities in which they're located while still maintaining profitability for stakeholders. Can companies do both? Of course they can. More than that, they should, for their own interests.

Creating a balance between the needs of stakeholders and the needs of the community is no more than an extension of ethical corporate behavior. And good ethical corporate behavior enhances corporate image, generates both employee and consumer loyalty, and fosters wide support among shareholders and suppliers. Those who may pooh-pooh these kinds of values and tar them with phrases such as "socialism" are missing the point. More than that, they are missing the opportunity to improve general performance and future prospects for the firm.

Developing a code of ethical business practices in a large corporation can involve an extended series of meetings over many months or even years to produce a small library of revisions, followed by a launch ceremony that is heavy with pride and principle. It's all unnecessary, because the entire range of ethical standards tends to be a direct reflection of the founder's or leader's values.

Too often, a company's ethics are measured by words alone—words enshrined in the firm's code of ethics. But remember how effective Enron's sixty-plus pages of ethical standards were in ensuring its good behavior? Words never achieve anything of substance without deeds to back them up.

The important thing is to put ethical principles into action, to *live* those corporate values every day, throughout the organization. Values-driven leadership means setting the standards from the top, modeling ethical behavior for everyone in the company, and fostering a culture of doing business in a principled way.

In a slightly different context but with an identical philosophy, the great Roman general and philosopher Marcus Aurelius provided all the guidance needed to raise America's business ethics when he preached two thousand years ago (and please forgive the gender-specific reference): *Waste no time arguing about what a good man is. Be one!*

I HAVE SPENT several thousand words to this point telling you and America how debased our ethical standards have become in the sphere of business, especially in the Trump era, and what happens when there is such a gap. Now it's time for me to show there is a better way, and to explain how to conduct business according to ethical standards—not just to do the right thing, but also to improve results and performance by any measure.

But first, we'll start Part Two by getting personal. This is where I share with you my own story to explain why doing business in a responsible, principled way is so important to me, and how it can make a big difference for you, too.

Here is where moralizing ends and storytelling begins.

PART TWO

From Tar-Paper Shack to Paneled Boardroom

8

How Do You Know When You're Wealthy?

MUCH HAS BEEN made of Donald Trump's beginnings as the son of a prominent, wealthy and, according to many who knew him, domineering father. Trump generated a good deal of mockery when, while attempting to downplay his roots and enhance his achievements, he explained that he got his start in business when his father gave him "a small loan of a million dollars."[37] He was also privileged to have received his grounding in economics at the prestigious Wharton School of Business.

I neither resent the advantage that his family's wealth provided him nor attach any blame for Trump's ethical shortcomings to it. Many young people in America have failed terribly in business and in life despite the benefits of family wealth and paid education. And, of course, many of America's great business leaders can trace their success back to much humbler beginnings that include poverty, abuse and deprivation.

In fact, the story I am about to recount of my modest background and my subsequent success in business reads like the classic rags-to-riches American tale (except that mine started in Canada). I grew up in a tar-paper shack in northern Ontario and ended up presiding over paneled boardrooms in California and elsewhere in the United States. I am no different than Donald Trump in pursuing the American dream. And I am as proud as Trump, I suspect, of the distance I have traveled in terms of financial security and material success. So why contrast my background with Trump's? Because my journey, and my view of that ideal, are entirely different from his.

The comparison has nothing to do with material envy. I believe that to fully understand the significance of values and ethics, and to fully appreciate their importance, it helps to grasp their origins. Are we born with a sense of fairness and ethical behavior? Or are we taught them in the same manner as we are taught other appropriate conduct, from toilet training to table manners? Whether nature, nurture or both, in my journey through business and life I have learned much about applying my aptitudes and directing my ambitions while being fair in my relationships with clients, employees, communities and family.

And I'm still learning. In fact, one of the most dramatic lessons was delivered by my eight-year-old son at a time when I was wallowing in disappointment instead of celebrating success. It was a classic example of being so inwardly focused on my own pain that I could not recognize the pain that others were feeling... and that I had inadvertently caused.

I'M NOT A great reader of fiction, but I know that one of the best opening sentences in English literature is from Charles Dickens' *A Tale of Two Cities*. The words define a major turning point in my life: "It was the best of times, it was the worst of times..." That's how I felt the night that I sat in my eight-year-old son's bedroom, reading him a story.

It had been about a year since I had sold Sheppard Associates, the company I had founded fifteen years earlier on nothing more than ambition and experience. The global organization that acquired it paid me more money than I once thought was in the entire world. My company would remain an entity within the parent corporation, and I could earn substantially more money through an "earn-out" deal, which involved remaining in charge and building the volume of business. So, with company stock as a first payment earning me money, I set to work earning more.

We were headquartered in Glendale, California, with branches in Atlanta, Boston, Chicago, Houston, Minneapolis, Portland and Stamford (Connecticut). Our parent company client list included major corporations such as 3M, Disney, SBC Communications, Levi Strauss & Co., Brown & Root/Halliburton, Shell Oil, Reebok, Boeing, Avery Dennison, U.S. Bancorp, MediaOne and Sun Microsystems. As the largest independent full-service employee communication firm in the country, working within the framework of the much larger umbrella firm that had bought the business, we were poised to expand at an enormous rate, which would produce an even fatter payday for me. The earn-out arrangement encouraged me to keep doing what I had been doing for more than thirty years while leveraging the substantial size, reach and depth of support from the parent company, adding millions of dollars to my assets. If I could grow the business by working as hard for the new owners as I had worked on my own, I could more than double the initial price they had paid me.

Naturally, I set to work with more energy than ever. I became a whirlwind of travel, meetings, presentations and pitches, driving myself and everyone associated with me to higher levels of achievement day after day. Somewhere down the road was another major payday for me. Or so I thought.

In case you haven't heard it before, let me tell you that there is a vast difference between entrepreneurs and managers. They're not just two different kinds of businesspeople. They are two different species of animal. No one then running Ketchum Inc., the new parent of Sheppard Associates, had ever launched a business, working sixteen or eighteen hours a day and agonizing over expenses and cash flow, waking at three in the morning to worry about the bank loan and wonder how they would pay the staff salaries that month. They may have been decent managers, and I'm sure at least a few of them boasted MBAs from good schools. But entrepreneurs are born, not made, and all the MBAs and good schools in America won't turn a manager into a risk-taker.

BREAKING NEWS: Not Everyone Thinks Like an Entrepreneur

I had spent my entire working career with an entrepreneurial frame of mind. Even when employed by giants like Mercer and Johnson & Higgins before founding my own firm, I had thought like an entrepreneur. Which meant I was focused on building the business, taking calculated risks, and counting the profits I generated. It made setting out on my own, when I launched Sheppard Associates, a fairly smooth move.

My arrangement with the new owners reflected that mind-set. But only on paper. The promise was clear: I would bring an entrepreneurial attitude to building the business and be rewarded for the growth I generated. But I would be the sole direct beneficiary of all my effort. The deal had been an incentive for me to sell my company. "Here's half the money," the buyers said in effect. "Pull in a raft of new business and we'll give you more. A lot more." There would be a pot of gold waiting for me somewhere down the road, and everyone knew the contents of the pot would be mine, not theirs.

My efforts to rake in new business for the company involved lighting a fire under some of my new associates, and these efforts were met with resistance—a lot of resistance. Why should they work as hard as me for that pot of gold, tossing aside their bureaucratic attitude and assuming the ambition of a driven entrepreneur like me? What, after all, was in it for them? Tension built between us until, barely a year after I signed the deal to sell my company, two senior members of my team cornered me one day. We needed, they said, to have a talk. A firm, private and honest talk.

As it turned out, they did most of the talking and I did most of the listening. They explained that my efforts to hit my target were disruptive. They understood my ambition and how I operated (they had worked with me for several years and they knew I threw myself totally into work), but I was making their lives miserable by striving to corral new business while pulling a giant bureaucratic organization along with me. No one was happy, including (I had to admit) me. We exchanged views, shared suggestions and shed a few tears together. In the end, I got their message: It would be best for all if I left.

And so I did. I walked away from my company and career, leaving millions of potential dollars on the table. I found myself unemployed for the first time in my adult life, with neither the prospects nor the need to work for a living. I sat in my beautiful Southern California home and reviewed where I was, how far I had come and what I had achieved. On the surface it was all good. I had a wonderful wife, two lovely young children and a fat bank account. It was the American dream come true.

Did I feel wealthy, successful and satisfied? No. I felt like a failure. I had built my identity and measured my worth as a human being by my success at building my own company and selling it for a large sum of cash. My company was gone. And gone with it, I believed, was my sense of who I was and what I stood for.

Besides that, those years of building a successful business had come with a price that all of us paid—my wife, our children and me. I had not been home often enough to appreciate and admire the house that Cayce and I owned. More to the point, I hadn't been around enough to fully appreciate her or our children or even get to know them as well as I should.

Finding the Measure of Success in a Bedtime Story

One evening I took a break from wallowing in my sense of failure and decided to do something I had done rarely in the past—something most parents do as a matter of course: read my son, Malone, a story before bedtime.

I can't remember anything about the story or the book I was reading it from. But I will never forget my shock at realizing that Malone, snuggled against me on the sofa, was crying. When I asked him why he was so sad he replied, "I'm not sad. I'm just happy that you're here, reading a story to me."

I realized in that moment that for years my son believed I had been away from home so often because I didn't want to be with him. The realization hit me with tremendous power. The more I thought of Malone's words, the more I considered that my choice to walk away from the money I might have made was a gift from God. All the things that seemed important to me a week earlier—driving myself and others to score a new success at business and earn millions of dollars to bolster my ego but not my happiness—were secondary to that moment with my son.

The common term for this, I suppose, is epiphany or revelation. Both terms have religious connotations, and that's fine with me. Until that point in my life, I had not consciously visualized God's hand in my own. I had no clear sense of a higher power that guides us through life if we heed the clues. Things changed that evening.

I still could take pride in all I had achieved in my business career. I could remind myself how far I had traveled from my childhood, how many lives I had influenced for the better, how successful I was by material measures. I had no reason to regret my work to that point. I began, however, to sense a need to shift my priorities away from work and money. In the long run, something else mattered much more.

My most significant measure of my identity became my family. I wanted them to know that I preferred to share my time, my energy and my life with them. That idea of family as the first priority may seem, on the surface at least, entirely normal for most people who spent their childhood in a warm and nurturing family environment. But, as I'll explain later, I had not been so fortunate, and the concept needed more effort from me to make it reality.

My next priority involved friends. Laughter, companionship and trust are the measures of a good life, and the source of them all are our relationships with people whose opinions we value and who inspire mutual respect. Third came my community. I'm not much interested in hermits and I've never been interested in becoming one. Happy people engage in their community and extend that bond beyond their immediate neighborhood.

I live in La Cañada, a mostly white, upscale suburb of Los Angeles. I love everything about it—the location, the climate, the setting, the schools and much more. I began looking beyond La Cañada to all the regions around us—Pasadena, Glendale and other parts of Greater Los Angeles. Most of them, I realized, lacked many things I had taken for granted. I saw poverty, racial tension and widespread frustration. What I failed to see in these less affluent areas was the outlook for many children to find the kind of joy in their lives that they deserved.

I'm not certain if my son's joy at discovering he had a father who cared for him, or the memory of my own difficult childhood, made the bigger impact on me, but I related to those kids. Many had no opportunity to share in games and organized sports. They didn't know what it was like to compete as a team, discovering both the immense joy of winning and the comfort of sharing the heartbreak of loss.

Los Angeles is a wonderful city in many ways, and I felt fortunate to live there. I still feel that way. But for many Hispanic, African-American and other minority kids, they didn't feel nearly as lucky. Climate, location and other qualities of L.A. life were just as available to them, but opportunity, equality, education and security were scarce.

Long before Donald Trump spoke of Hispanics as though they were unwanted pests, I understood the plight of the children living in and around Los Angeles. I wanted to assist them in some meaningful way, and I did.

My act of charity cost me in many ways. The price included the near loss of the marriage and family that represented much of who I was and what I valued in my life. How did I arrive at a place where I had so much to celebrate by one measure and so much to lose by another?

To answer this, I need to begin at a distant time and place. Like over fifty years ago. In a location that I don't believe could be in sharper contrast with my current home in the San Gabriel Valley.

THE TERRAIN SURROUNDING the town where I grew up was once so desolate, so lacking in vegetation, that it was chosen by NASA as a training site for Apollo astronauts bound for a moon landing.

One of the Apollo mission objectives had been to locate meteorite strikes on the moon's surface, and the billion-year-old rock surface of the Sudbury Basin in northern Ontario, Canada, qualified perfectly. The basin itself, about forty miles wide, was created about 2 billion years ago from the impact of a continent-sized meteor or comet. No one seems to be sure which it was, but the long-ago impact left the area rich in copper and nickel ore. Today the land is barren, the air temperature is often chilly, and for several years you could travel miles without encountering evidence of plant or animal life.*

I mention this because we never realize how much we are shaped by all the influences of our childhood until we are mature enough to look back at them from a distant perspective. Things grow clear with time. We recognize the way our values were fixed, we understand the emotions we felt back then, and we realize how they echo within us today. If our lives have proved satisfying and beneficial to others, we can even feel grateful for the pain, losses, disappointments and setbacks we endured. My years growing up in Sudbury were never easy, although I found joy and a sense of accomplishment in them. The biggest impact they had on me was the knowledge that life can be a challenge, not a joyride, and that the best way to meet challenges is to be tough and persistent. You don't get anywhere in life by giving up or by hoping that things will get better. If you want things to improve, it's up to you to make them better. Kids have been given similar advice for generations. Some heed it, others ignore it. Being raised as I was, and *where* I was, left me no choice—if I wanted to improve my lot in life, the only person I could count on doing it... was me.

I have lived in Southern California for almost forty years. I married the kind of California girl that the Beach Boys wrote songs about, helped raise our children here, and luxuriate in the California sunshine. The bleak landscape from my childhood now seems as distant as the moon itself. But I am here in part because of the things I witnessed and learned as a child in that northland. My modest upbringing also encouraged me to work as hard as—and even harder than—the people around me. Working hard at whatever I did was the only way I knew to achieve the kind of life I wanted to live.

* Much of the barren nature of the area was heightened by settlers who stripped whatever vegetation they could locate for firewood. Through much of the twentieth century, heavy concentrations of acid rain limited new growth of vegetation. Over the years since then, much of the land has changed; planted seedlings have grown into mature trees, and the region is more attractive and less moonlike.

A Good Place to Come From

If you know where Duluth, Minnesota, is on a map, imagine drawing a line due east from there. Stretch the line about five hundred miles and you'll arrive at Sudbury. When I was born in the late 1940s the city's population was about forty thousand, equally split between French Canadians and English-speaking residents of various origins—mostly English, Scottish, Irish, German, Italian and a few First Nations people. The men worked in mines, digging and hauling up nickel and copper ore from deep in the ground. The women stayed home cooking, washing, ironing and having babies. Lots of babies.

I was one of eight children, born just after the end of World War II. My father had shipped overseas in the Canadian Army when the war began. This may make him sound like a war hero, but he wasn't. He remained in England, driving trucks and ambulances, eating good meals and hanging out with his buddies. Whenever he talked about the war he would say those were the best years of his life. For a guy who had left school at age twelve to work at cutting timber in lumber camps and at hard-rock mining, they probably were.

My family was living in my grandmother's small tar-paper shack when I was born in the city of North Bay. We moved from there to converted army barracks, then to an apartment over a pool hall and later to a relative's basement. When my father took a permanent mining job in Sudbury we headed there, settling into a small three-room house with no running water and an outhouse in the back. The winters in Sudbury are cold, almost unbelievably cold to a native Californian, with temperatures rarely crawling above 0°F for weeks. Summers are short and often steaming through July and August. It is a land of extremes in many ways.* It was a tough climate, a tough place to live, and our home wasn't much different.

All children need models more than they need critics. Fathers, according to the stereotypes of the 1950s, were supposed to serve as models of strength and courage, someone their children could rely

* The city has spawned a number of people who left Sudbury for greener pastures. The host of *Jeopardy*, Alex Trebek, is from Sudbury. So is Farhan Zaidi, the current general manager of the Los Angeles Dodgers, and (no surprise here) at least eighty-one players in the NHL.

upon to teach them how to deal with other people and show them respect. My father was not one of those people. I saw him as a coward and a bully, a man who related more to his union "brothers" than to his own family. He treated my mother as though she didn't exist, never showing her any sign of affection, never giving her a hint of independence or pride. If other women were present, he became charming and sociable, eager to impress them with his personality. It was all a sham.

Over the years I began to understand my father, even if I could not find it in myself to admire him. His lack of a proper upbringing, his deplorable home life and his work in the mines destroyed whatever gentleness may have been within him. Trudging in darkness a mile or more underground day after day, with little hope of change or improvement in conditions or take-home pay, will do that to you. During sub-zero winter months the men descended in darkness, labored in darkness and returned home in darkness. Things were made worse by the two organizations that dictated my father's life and the lives of almost every resident in the area: the mining company and the union.

My father worked for Falconbridge Nickel Mines Limited. Mining companies rarely have good long-term relationships with their workers, and this one was no exception. Falconbridge operated company stores, where employees purchased overpriced food and clothing between paydays, their debt subtracted from their biweekly paychecks. Little cash was left over—just enough for beer and cigarettes in many cases.

Like many people in the area, we owned a large freezer. In fact, it was one of our most prized appliances. Why a freezer in such a northern climate? Because it helped us eat better. Beyond the desolate Sudbury Basin, the woods teemed with wildlife, especially moose and deer. In hunting season men would head into the brush, dragging out a carcass to be butchered, yielding a hundred or more pounds of meat to supplement groceries from the company stores. The meat was generally tough and gamey. Most people, including my mother, never served it as a roast or steaks. It was ground like hamburger, then packaged and frozen to be consumed in lean months. Grinding it in that manner made it palatable, especially when baked into meat pies, a special treat at Christmas.

From time to time the miners would go on strike, launching long bitter periods when families survived on welfare and strike pay from the unions. The walkouts often lasted for months with neither the union nor the company budging. Falconbridge management, anticipating the strike, would ramp up production, stockpile the ore and continue selling it while the mine sat closed and the workers paraded with hand-lettered signs, shouting empty slogans while they and their families tried to scrape by on handouts.

My father worshipped the unions. I felt differently. Unions, I concede, played a role in improving working conditions—as much improvement as you can offer men working eight or ten hours a day in near-darkness, breathing potentially deadly dust, handling acid, fearing that the rock walls and ceilings would collapse upon them any moment. I eventually viewed the actions of unions and their leaders as unfair and evil as the mine company and its managers. During extended strikes, union leaders continued to receive the same high salaries while the workers and their families scrimped and sought welfare assistance. I grew to suspect that the unions and Falconbridge management colluded with each other, agreeing on settlements before negotiations began. The miners would strike for several weeks, even months, finally settling for an increase of maybe 10 cents an hour. It would take years to recover the losses they suffered during the strike and to pay the debt they had built up. When the new contract expired, they would face the prospect of yet another strike. I remember thinking there had to be a better way for employers and workers to get along.

It seemed to me that if the mining companies viewed their employees as the source of the firm's wealth rather than an expense to be tolerated, both sides would have benefited. Strikes were and are costly to everyone. The companies lose production, the workers lose income, each side loses trust in the other, and the cost to the community is measured in anger and tension. Growing up in a unionized mining household I was exposed to all the damages created not just by strikes but by the simmering rage of the miners who were being cruelly exploited by management. I disliked the unions and the company leaders with equal measure, and for similar reasons. Both sides needed each other to succeed, I knew, so why couldn't they find a way to work together?

Of course, I never sat in a Falconbridge boardroom or office and listened to managers and executives discuss the actions of the unions. But I'd had enough exposure to the unions to understand how they worked and what they stood for.

Competition Among Labor Brotherhoods

Falconbridge was a cash cow, not just for its shareholders and the community surrounding it, but also for the unions representing its workers. Two different unions competed for the right to act for miners at Falconbridge and other operations, especially the right to collect union dues from them. My father belonged to the Union of Mine, Mill and Smelter Workers, which fought off the United Steelworkers union, who claimed to do a better job of improving working conditions.

The fierce competition between the rival unions caused the miners to lose sight of the big picture. Instead of seeing the mining company as the common enemy and exploring ways to confront management directly about its unfair practices without depending on the unions, the miners placed their faith entirely in the unions, who were too caught up with their own power struggle to represent the miners. In fact, so competitive were the two unions that the miners viewed them as opposing teams in some strange professional sports league, identifying with one or the other. But they weren't like sports fans. They were more like members of street gangs, thugs who would threaten members of rival gangs, handing out beatings to anyone foolish enough to wander into another neighborhood not their own.

I can recall my father's union buddies showing up at our house on a Saturday night, sitting around and drinking beer, grumbling about their work and their lives until someone would raise a fist and shout, "Let's go get us some steelworkers!" The others would stand and yell their support, some saying they'd get baseball bats as weapons and others displaying razorblades embedded in the toes of their work boots, prepared to kick an unfortunate union rival to death or at least to unconsciousness.

They would storm into the night, my mother and the rest of us glad to see them leave. Often they would return an hour or two later, talking about what they could've done, would've done, should've done had they encountered any steelworkers, my father pleading with my mother to make sandwiches for his friends.

I found nothing of value in their antics. I understood my father worked hard in dangerous and difficult conditions and that his work paid for the food that I ate and the clothes on my back. I also understood why they acted that way. Their anger and frustration ran deep, and they needed a way to vent it so they could retain some dignity and pride. But it all seemed wrong—the policies of the mining company, the exploitation of the employees by both the company and the union, the silly posturing of the men to express their anger, and above all their general lack of decency in the way some treated their wives and children.

Despite the dangers of mining and the unfair treatment by the mining companies, most of the boys I knew at school couldn't wait to get a job in the mines. It was a macho way to work and it paid relatively well. It was what real men did in that part of the world at that time. And it was all they really knew.

I had no intention of earning my living a mile underground, breathing harmful dust and cursing both my employer and my union. Becoming the kind of person my father had become: bitter, resentful, hopeless and distant. I wanted out of mining and away from Sudbury. But first I had to deal with my own anger and resentment.

I found my release and my ticket out by playing sports and by excelling at schoolwork.

The Price—and Pain—of Being a Rebel

I achieved good (but not great) school marks with little effort. I was bright enough to understand the lessons, and school represented a warm and rewarding alternative to my home life. I enjoyed the classroom environment, although it wasn't always encouraging. In fact, thanks to the corporal punishments handed out in public schools at the time, it was often painful. I worked only hard enough to get by in my school studies. I didn't do my homework and rarely studied for exams. The teachers knew I had the potential to do much better if I chose to work harder. But instead of searching for a positive way of encouraging me, they applied physical force in a manner that would get them arrested today. They believed far more in the stick than the carrot. In public school I was strapped on the hands many times for breaking one rule or another, or for not showing enough deference to my superiors. My high school math teacher broke a clipboard over my head, my history teacher threw me against a wall in frustration and a phys ed teacher stood me against a wall while he kicked volleyballs at me. My Latin teacher took a less physical approach; she constantly screamed at me like a banshee.

If my resistance to their punishments and my failure to comply with their demands sound like classic rebellious schoolboy behavior, then I guess I was a rebel. Now I see it as immaturity plus adolescent anger and frustration at much of life around me—my father's bullying manner, our poverty that made items like fresh fruits and vegetables an often-unaffordable luxury, the fear that I might spend my life working in the mines, the long bitter winters, and more. Poverty and constant abuse polarize people. The effect can be crushing, leaving them convinced that they will never compete, never rise above living hand to mouth and being victims. Or it can both toughen and stimulate them, creating a reservoir of anger and a determination to never let poverty or circumstances or other people crush them economically.

I don't recall feeling like a victim. I do remember, however, feeling angry at things I couldn't control in my life.

My anger was aimed at the kids around me as much as authority figures. Despite my small size, I never backed away from a fight, and often looked for one just to prove how tough I was. Eventually no one wanted to mess with me, and among some of the kids I acquired the nickname Super Don. Today I suppose I would be called a Bad Ass.

When my reputation as a local tough guy grew, I discovered I didn't need to prove anything—just threatening to fight someone was enough for the other guy to back down.

I acted differently with my brothers and sisters. I protected them against abuse from my father, and played a parent's role with my younger brothers, taking them fishing and doing other things like buying my young brother Dale his first bicycle.

In the middle of this turmoil I managed to do something that no one in my family had achieved before: I remained in school past grade 10, intent on graduating and attending college and university.

The other fortunate aspect of my youth was my interest in sports. Competitive sports became an outlet for my anger and energy. They also developed my leadership ability, especially when I played quarterback for our high school football team. I enjoyed taking charge, choosing the plays and watching us score against other school teams—which we did often enough to win the district championship for the first time in the school's history. Not bad for a kid who stood five-feet-seven-inches tall and weighed maybe 140 pounds.

I loved hockey even more. I loved the speed of the game, and the raw tough attitude and athleticism it demanded. Of all the sports I could have encountered in my youth, hockey suited me best. I was so good on the ice that my father began spinning dreams of me playing in the NHL, picturing me skating over the ice for the Toronto Maple Leafs, making pots of money a season and enabling him to say to his mine-worker buddies, "That's my son!"

I also played basketball, primarily because I could stay warm in the gym and avoid freezing my toes off outside in winter. In fact, the most attractive part of basketball was taking a hot shower after the game, before dressing and heading home. I loved hot showers. At home we took a hot bath now and then, only in water painstakingly heated, pail by pail, atop the wood-fired stove and poured into a galvanized metal tub. I had never had hot showers before playing basketball. They seemed like the height of luxury to me. This, I told myself, is how successful people live. Not with wood stoves and galvanized bathtubs but with hot water flowing freely from a shower whenever they wanted to take one—and with anything else they could dream up to add to their comfort.

Sports taught me something else as well. It taught me to play to win, and to play fair. You may have natural skill, as I had in hockey, but I soon learned that skill alone didn't guarantee a championship ring or even a spot on the team. You achieved success by working harder than anyone else and playing within the rules. Those were the first lessons for me in sports, and I have managed to carry them over to both business and my personal life.

The End of School and Family Life

High school became my source of happiness when I was in the higher grades. The joy of playing sports, the fun at school dances, the thrill of meeting beautiful girls who found me attractive and interesting. Those memories balance the darker side of my life at the time, and I treasure them.

The only thing that troubled me in my final months of high school was the next step for me to take in life. Would graduation mean the end of my formal education? The beginning of a whole new outlook on life from attending college? Or something totally unexpected? I knew only this for sure: I would find a way to enjoy a life that included all the hot showers I wanted to take. And I would never go to work in the mines.

I had been enrolled in the high school collegiate course, a five-year program that extended to grade 13, preparing graduates for college studies. My father, perhaps in acknowledgment of my achievement at remaining in school past grade 10, expected me to find a way into college and emerge with a degree of some kind. But something happened near the end of the school year to change everything.

Over lunch a few days before graduation, I heard one of the boys in my class brag that he planned to get a job with a company downtown. He would be working in a big modern office building, far from the Falconbridge mines. He would wear a jacket and tie every day and even have a job title: Branch Secretary Trainee.

The idea of working in an office, dressing in nice clothes, and having an impressive-sounding title—even if I didn't know what it meant—was too tempting to ignore. The boy who was bragging about his job ambitions had no more right to a position like that than me, I reasoned. That afternoon I headed downtown to the biggest office I could find. The company was Manufacturers Life, or Manulife. I walked in, asked to see the manager, introduced myself and asked if he had an opening for a branch secretary trainee, whatever that was. He said he did, and he began asking me questions about my background and ambition. When I answered all his questions with confidence, I was offered the position at a salary of $37 a week. And I was told to start work the very next day.

At home that night, I broke the news to my family, explaining that I would earn a weekly paycheck, work in a modern office, wear a shirt and tie every day and have an impressive title. I was proud of myself for having landed such a good job and my prospects for a brilliant business career.

I don't recall the reactions of my mother or my siblings. I never forgot the dark look on my father's face and his angry words to me. "If you're smart enough to get a job and take care of yourself," he snapped, "then get the hell out of here!"

I did. The very next day.

9

When They Need You More than You Need Them

I MADE JUST ENOUGH money in my first job to take a room in a boarding house on the edge of town before finding a tiny basement apartment of my own. Between paying the rent, taking the bus to work and back and covering other expenses, there was little left of my salary at the end of the week. Whenever I went home for a visit, my mother would hand me food to survive on for a few days.

On a more encouraging note, I had a girlfriend, my lovely childhood sweetheart from high school. Her name was Sylvia, and whenever I visited her home, Sylvia's mother saw how difficult things were for this ambitious seventeen-year-old kid and would give me food to take home as well. I survived on the generosity and nurturing of mothers—mine and Sylvia's.

I needed ambition, because there wasn't much else to carry me through my workday. Manulife was a giant life insurance firm headquartered in Toronto, but there were only two functions for people working at the Sudbury office. One was to process and file details on policyholders, ensuring that premiums were paid and that accurate records were kept. Directing this task was the responsibility of the branch secretary, a role I was being prepared to assume some day. The other function was to support the sales staff, who worked under the branch manager and filled the most important duties: they brought in business. Watching the salespeople and absorbing their techniques taught me an early lesson about business ethics.

Most life insurance was sold door-to-door back then, and it was a difficult way to make a living. Buying coverage on your life or on the life of your spouse was a little like visiting the dentist—you knew it was good for you, but it cost money and there were no immediate benefits. Which made it a real challenge to show up on someone's doorstep and talk him or her into a sale. There was always a need for good life insurance salespeople. And there was never a long-term supply of them.

Until they actually attempted it, to most people selling insurance seemed like a great career. The commissions were good, and they kept paying off. For years after you made a sale, commissions flowed your way as long as the policyholders kept paying their premiums.

Many people—all of whom were young men at the time—were attracted to the idea of being a life insurance salesman. Manulife, like other insurance companies, encouraged them. They provided basic sales training before sending the recruits out into the world to sell insurance policies.

The beginnings were almost always promising. The new salesman would launch his career with relatives and friends, pitching the benefits of life insurance to people his own age who were married (or considering it) and starting a family (or considering it). Buying life insurance coverage was almost a rite of passage, an acceptance of responsibility as an adult. And buying it from a sibling or a neighbor or a buddy made it even more appealing. So the first dozen or so policy sales were usually easy.

The next dozen—in fact, the rest of the new salesperson's career—were less than easy. They were almost impossible. Reaching beyond their immediate circle of contacts to make a sale meant cold-calling, interrupting a stranger's life to sell something the prospect didn't intend to buy until you came along. Cold calls are the root canal procedures of selling. The pleasures are few and far between, and the word heard most often is a direct "No!"

After a rousing first few months in the business, many people decided that selling life insurance wasn't their ticket to wealth and security after all. (Admittedly, a small minority of sales trainees discovered they had the work ethic needed to sell effectively, and most of them did well.) With such a steady turnover, motivating existing sales staff and recruiting new members proved a demanding task for a branch manager.

I can't pin any unethical behavior on one person. But I recall the pressure that new salespeople felt once they had exhausted their contacts among family and friends and were faced with making cold calls. How did they deal with buyer resistance? What did they say in reply to "I don't want any"? I believed in insurance, especially where families were concerned. But I knew that insurance salespeople often went to great lengths to make the sale and keep their job. Did they lie to do it? Would they stretch the truth to put money in their own pockets? And if they did, how would they feel about it later? Was selling really a dog-eat-dog situation?

Good salespeople don't need to lie or stretch the truth. They need training and an ability to relate to people. If they have both those things, ethics and values don't really enter the picture. I've understood this through my entire career, and it has made me impatient with anyone who scoffs at the sales professional and assumes all successful salespeople, by definition, are unscrupulous.

It is not at all true. We need to recognize that selling plays a vital role in every aspect of business. I recall seeing a framed sign hanging on a wall in a sales manager's office. The sign said: NOTHING HAPPENS UNTIL SOMEBODY SELLS SOMETHING. In a book dealing with business ethics, it's important to remind everyone of that fact.

My responsibilities in that early job didn't involve sales. I spent most of my time filing documents, running the mimeograph machine and entering client information onto punch cards, the forerunners of digital computer data storage. Back then it was basic grunt work in an office. All the women in the office were more senior than me, usually telling me what to do, how to do it and when to have it done. But in those days, my future was brighter than theirs—as a male, I was being groomed for management responsibilities. Fortunately, things have changed somewhat for the better for women.

Applying the Power of Smarts

My energy made an impression on Merv Patterson, manager of the Sudbury branch. Like all mentors, he saw something in me that others missed, and he believed that I had a future well beyond filing. Better than that, he chose to do something about it. Merv knew I was struggling financially. He would invite me to have lunch with him, picking up the check to save me a few bucks and making sure I had some nourishment. He even paid for my haircuts now and then. Most valuable of all, he gave me some advice that still resonates with me today.

"Donnie," he said once, "when people look at you, they can't tell if you're smart, but they can see how hard you work. Keep working harder than anybody else, and eventually your smarts will take you past them all."

Hearing those words as a seventeen-year-old kid who, for most of his life, had been told his future would be in the nickel mines, provided more encouragement than I can measure, even now. I worked until past seven o'clock every night, signed up for every training course available, read every job hint the company offered and watched every move made by the best people in the company. Looking back at that period, it's as though I had been some kind of thoroughbred racehorse locked in the starting gate. When Merv Patterson opened it for me, I was off and running down the track, straining to stay ahead of the field.

It paid off. Within a year, I was moved to the Manulife branch in Calgary, Alberta. I was still a branch secretary trainee, but the Calgary branch was much larger and in a far more sophisticated city.

Manulife had plans for me. I flew, for the first time, across the Prairies to the Rocky Mountains at Manulife's expense. The company even covered the cost of my first few nights in a Holiday Inn until I got my bearings and found an apartment.

The job promotion, such as it was, went to my head, literally. I bought a fedora and an umbrella, on the assumption that both were essential for a future executive's wardrobe. I may have been an eighteen-year-old trainee, but I began posing as a thirty-something executive. Which led to problems from time to time. Like the time a bunch of guys at the office, all of them members of the Jaycees, invited me to join them at a Junior Chamber of Commerce cocktail party.

When the bartender asked what I'd like to drink, I had to think about it for a moment. The only alcohol I had consumed to that point was the Manhattan offered me on the flight to Calgary, and it had tasted terrible. I didn't want another one of those, so I recalled the cool, sophisticated drinks I'd seen executives consume in movies and on TV dramas. Two came to mind: Scotch and soda, and gin and tonic. With the older guys watching, I swallowed my panic and ordered a Scotch and tonic. When the others stopped laughing, they wouldn't let me drink the concoction and I realized I had a lot to learn before I could feel totally comfortable as "a young man on the move."

My education developed in other, more practical ways. One bit of advice I acquired has served me far better than fedoras, umbrellas and alcohol: *Always be more important to your employers than they are to you.* I was still something of a renegade at heart, a young guy more determined than ever to succeed in the business world, but equally determined to do it my way whenever possible. The concept of building my value to an employer hadn't occurred to me, but the benefits eventually became obvious in a way that changed my career and life entirely.

Within a year of moving to Calgary, I began casting my eyes elsewhere. I wanted to return to Ontario, preferably Toronto, which was becoming a major financial and business center. The idea wasn't based entirely on improving my job situation. I was still in love with my high school girlfriend, Sylvia, and on two occasions I had ridden the train from Calgary to Sudbury, a journey that involved two days and two nights of rocking side to side in a railroad coach, sleeping sitting up and surviving on stale sandwiches, just to spend a couple of days with her. A job in Toronto would not only bring me closer to Sylvia—it would make my dream of marrying her, and making a home together, a reality. Perhaps.

Word got around Calgary that I was energetic, intelligent and ambitious, and all three qualities inspired Great-West Life, a major rival of Manulife, to offer me a position in their Toronto office. I accepted it with glee, and was off to Toronto within a week or two.

I stopped in Sudbury long enough to visit Sylvia and break the good news to my family. When I arrived, a message was waiting for me. My former boss at the Sudbury office of Manulife had called to say that a senior executive with Manulife was insisting that I stay with the company. As an incentive, he offered me a position at their corporate office, also in Toronto, in the company's group service department.

The proof of the advice I had picked up earlier landed right in front of me: I was more valuable to Manulife than they had been to me, and my reward was a major move forward in status, responsibilities and income.

There was so much more to learn, of course, and within days of landing in Toronto I began absorbing the lessons I encountered. Some were enlightening. Others were discouraging. A few, I decided, were simply dumb.

Chairs with Arms, Racks for Coats and Other Silly Rules

My first lesson was the so-called rule of bureaucratic status. My boss's office at Manulife corporate HQ was furnished with a visitor's chair and a coat rack. The visitor's chair had arms. Was that a big deal? Yes, it was. In the corporate world of the mid-60s, coat racks and chairs with arms symbolized your status within the company. Most managers' offices had armless chairs and no coat racks, and no one could claim such perks without being promoted to an appropriately elevated position. It seemed like nonsense to me at the time, and still does today. Contemporary businesses have more important things to measure than chair arms and coat racks in setting the status of middle managers.

I also began to grasp the Peter Principle, which was popular to quote among businesspeople at the time: "All managers rise to their own level of incompetence." The words were simultaneously amusing and wise, and I saw the principle practiced over and over during my first few weeks in my new position.

The best part of my job was the insight it gave me to an entirely new part of the insurance business. I was now beyond filing and distanced from cold-selling policies. Group Services dealt with employee benefit packages—disability insurance, pension plans and other products beyond life insurance alone.

I found this part of the business fascinating. I had never been aware of these products and services, and how they were developed and applied. I also began to appreciate the way some businesses assumed responsibility for assisting their employees when crises arose. It was a revelation to me, a contrast with the approach of the mining companies. I don't recall the extent to which Falconbridge and others went to assist their workers in bad times, and I suspect their efforts were always in response to demands from the unions. The companies I dealt with chose to offer their benefits as a means of attracting and keeping good employees, of course. But I believed the actions reflected their corporate values as well, and this was an eye-opener to me.

Learning about corporate values was encouraging, but working within the bureaucratic environment of the firm was often frustrating. Too many people, I saw, worked at minimal efficiency with equally minimal desire to succeed. Bureaucracies do not foster initiative, creativity or ambition. They tend to punish or restrict anyone who tries to break away from the pack, even to take the lead. I liked the company, I understood the work and I wanted to make the most of my opportunity. But I did not want to do it as a cog in a bureaucratic mechanism.

I recalled again the advice about being more valuable to my employer than my employer was to me. When I looked around to see who in the company was considered most valuable and best rewarded, I discovered it was the salespeople. They brought in the revenue that made the company profitable, after all. And salespeople had greater freedom in their work—as long as they met their quotas, they could avoid being tied down by silly bureaucratic rules and even fixed work hours. All that really counted was performance.

So I switched to sales, the most high-pressure, tension-filled job in the company. I took a position with a branch designated to familiarize new college graduates with the business. This made me a serious outlier. I had no degree, but I knew the guideline about being valuable to your employer, and how to make it pay off. I got my feet wet in sales, learned the process of selling, applied the techniques and made some impressive quotas. With that record established, I transferred to a more aggressive insurance agency, where exceeding your sales quota mattered more than toeing the bureaucratic line. It was a place where coat racks and chairs with arms didn't count; results did.

I had had no sales training and no experience at the beginning. What I had gained from working at head office for eighteen months or so was an insight into aspects of the company's products and services, and it gave me a serious advantage in my new sales role. It also forced me to deal with questions of ethical behavior that had bothered me earlier. I wanted to succeed as much as ever, but I refused to abandon my respect for openness and honesty. No one during my sales training, of course, suggested I lie or stretch the truth to close a sale. But everyone knew there would be opportunities to do so when dealing with prospects.

My defense against that dubious tactic was to view the products and services I sold not as items to be pushed on people like widgets, but rather as solutions for customers that they would understand and value. The secret would be to present them with the customer, not the salesman, in mind. That's Selling 101 in any training course you can name, but it's still news to a lot of people. You don't sell for yourself; you bury your ego and greed, and you sell for the customer first. It's honest and ethical. More than that, it's effective.

Here's an example: Many people owned insurance policies with large cash balances. Those owners of a certain age would be better off by converting their policies to annuities. I knew how to convince them to make the switch, and that every conversion was a commissioned sale. Policy owners thanked me profusely for improving their financial situation; I thanked them silently for improving my financial status. It all proved successful enough to qualify me as a member of the Million Dollar Round Table in my first year of sales.

I don't want to make this sound easy, because it wasn't. Like everyone else in sales, I had to make cold calls. I managed to achieve some success, but it was still rough slogging most of the time, and I grew prepared to hear "No," no matter how good my pitch might be. I might have stayed in sales and done well, but other aspects of the business began to attract me.

Big Business, Big Principles, Big Lessons

By this time, in the early 1970s, computers had ceased to be curiosities and were becoming necessities for many industries—including insurance. Desktop personal computers were still years away, but companies with mainframe units were busy developing programs to provide unique services for clients. One of those companies, a U.S.-based firm called Benefacts, prepared and distributed computerized employee benefits statements. Subscribing to the service enabled companies with large numbers of employees to distribute personalized reports to employees with a running account of the dollar value of the benefits provided for them, along with details of the benefits themselves. This doesn't sound like a big deal today, when the world is flooded with personalized computer printouts, but at the time it was a revolutionary concept.

Benefacts was searching for a Canadian sales representative. I applied, won the job and, at age twenty-one, found myself in a position with enormous growth possibilities, freedom to set my own schedule, a salary level I had never dreamed was possible and—wonder of wonders—a company car.

The job could have been designed especially for me. Or vice versa. I had the background, the knowledge, the skill sets and the drive to run with a revolutionary idea and make it work. It worked so well that I was soon contacted by William M. Mercer Limited, a giant pension and benefits consulting firm. Mercer wanted in on the benefits communication business. Benefacts was making big waves in that field, and Mercer chose to begin its foray into the benefits communication business with someone who could deliver sales. That turned out to be me.

Mercer wasn't just a giant in employee benefits planning. It was also the most aggressive, most prestigious company in the business. If it had been selling jewelry, it would have been Tiffany's, assuming Tiffany's emphasized high-powered sales as much as high-quality diamonds. Three things counted above all at Mercer. One was client service. Happy clients were the cornerstone of Mercer's business. Next came billings, or revenue. The biggest revenue producers in the company were treated like royalty. The third key to the company's success was its high ethical standards. Mercer dealt with some of the biggest corporations in North America, and these companies did not want to be associated with even a whiff of disreputable behavior.

The combination of fixed values and actual business practices made a major impression on me. I learned important lessons during my years at Mercer. They included not only how to be profitable *and* do business in a principled way, but also how to be profitable *as a result of* being an ethical business. In later years I analyzed Mercer's approach and adapted a version for my own business strategy: Put clients first; work hard to grow big; give no quarter to your competitors; outperform every opponent; and play fair.

If it sounds like my approach to playing hockey during those rough and tough games back in Sudbury, I'm sure it's not a coincidence. Playing hard and performing to win, all while playing by the rules and playing fair, is the way American business should operate. Not because it's some kind of moral imperative. But because it works.

You Can't Soar High without Ruffling a Few Feathers

Mercer* had grown into the largest benefits consultancy in the business based on service and referrals from satisfied clients. Like many

* Now a division of Marsh & McLennan.

prestigious companies, it invested little in promoting itself, an activity that seemed beneath such a haughty consulting firm. When it came to generating new accounts, Mercer assumed the attitude, "We're here, we're the best and everyone knows it. So why should we go looking for business?"

This presented a problem to me. Being aggressive in sales was the only way I knew how to operate. So I went to work making contacts, scheduling sales pitches and pulling in new clients. Mercer preferred to call the process "business development," but it was still sales to me and the rest of the world. The results impressed Mercer management so much that they instructed me to design a sales training course to be used within all departments in the Toronto head office. I began contracting people to write and produce videos, and I personally trained Mercer execs—most of them much older and more senior than me—on making calls, identifying key prospects, focusing on their needs and closing the sale. This approach may sound routine today, but back then it was quite groundbreaking. The training program I designed was based on sophisticated but well-known practices used by Manulife and other insurance companies. But no one had ever adapted them for Mercer.

Naturally, I ruffled a few feathers along the way. Based on the now-proven theory of becoming more valuable to your employers than they are to you, I figured I had nothing to lose. I promoted the near-scandalous idea that Mercer should take selling seriously and forget about the old ways of doing things "because we've always done them that way!" Fortunately, everyone of consequence in the company knew of the results I had achieved using the sales method I was teaching to others. When they realized it was still aligned with Mercer's ethical standards, they endorsed and adopted it, and the ruffled feathers were soon smoothed over.

My success earned me promotions, titles and salary increases. They were the obvious rewards. One benefit was less tangible but made a major impact on me. I realized that every success I achieved brought a growing sense of power my way. I became more valuable to my employer than my employer was to me, and I had managed to reach that stage even more effectively than in the past. Like so many lessons we learn in life, especially during the early years—I was still in my twenties—this one brought new realizations that I could apply in building my career and forging my business principles.

The first insight was that he or she who sets the pace in sales becomes royalty within the organization. Anyone can talk a good game in a sales office; the one who gets it done out in the field, however, takes home the biggest share of the gold. More than that, they earn genuine respect in the firm, from the boardroom down. Salespeople are the hunters and gatherers of business, the experienced pros who bring back trophy wins to the applause of everyone.

The second was understanding that breaking old policies is not the most important step in achieving success. For major leaps toward your target, you need to find new ways of doing business to replace them. This can be complex but enormously rewarding. Helping an organization to evolve in ways consistent with its past leads to advancing your own career and enhancing your leadership prospects.

The whole process was thrilling, it was satisfying, it was vengeance on everyone who had ever doubted me based on my modest origins and had scoffed at my ambitions. But it had its downside. Once I achieved a high level in the organization, there was no way for me to coast and ride with the tide for a while. Not that I wanted to—I loved what I was doing, and I thrived on the challenge of climbing as far up the ladder as I could go. This was fine for me. I was prepared—even anxious—to pay whatever price it took. The problem arose when I had to ask others to share the cost.

With my career on track, I married my high school sweetheart Sylvia, a warm and beautiful girl who took pride in all that I had achieved. We loved each other dearly, and in our way still do. We were both small-town kids who grew up with few expectations beyond having a roof over our heads and food on the table. Sylvia remained that way—her joy in life was spending time with me at dinner or a movie, or just relaxing at home. But I had changed. I was different from the kid who had fallen in love with her at high school. I had become a dragon slayer, a young guy from rough-and-tumble Sudbury intent on showing big-city types how to get things done, winning every battle and taking no prisoners. And I couldn't stop, any more than I could stop breathing. I accepted every chance, whatever it involved, to improve my value to the company.

For example, I had been terrified of speaking in public. But thanks to my success at Mercer I became noticed and was invited to speak at a major conference in Atlanta, Georgia. More than two thousand people, hosted by the International Foundation of Employee Benefit Plans, would wait for me to explain the secrets of benefits communication to them. I agreed to go without giving any thought to what I would say and how I would present it. This was a major step for me, because at heart I'm an introvert. I had never spoken to a group of more than a dozen or so, pitching a sale or teaching others the ins and outs of selling. This came easily to me, as it does to most salespeople.

Atlanta would be different. There would be no time to chat about the weather or discover personal interests together. If I accepted, I would be standing for half an hour in front of two thousand heavyweights in the business, trying to keep these total strangers interested in what I had to say. Logic and my reserved nature both told me to pass the invitation up. But I was ambitious as well as introverted, and my ambition had other things in mind.

Long before Nike popularized the line, I repeated to myself, "Just do it!" while working on the speech. And I did it. No one saw my knees shaking, and no one saw the grooves my clenched hands carved into the lectern. I finished the presentation to cheers and loud applause. The word echoed all the way back to Toronto: *Sheppard impressed the hell out of a massive audience in Atlanta! The guy's going places!*

Dominoes began to fall with that success. I was made a principal at Mercer and I hired a PR firm to book appearances for me on radio and TV, where I discussed the ins and outs of pensions and employee benefits. This upset folks at Mercer, but it didn't matter to me because it all paid off: America came calling.

On the first working day of 1980, the lowly kid from Sudbury was in California, assigned to launch and operate Mercer's benefits communication service out of San Francisco.

10

A New Way of Looking at Work

I EXPECTED THINGS TO change with my move to San Francisco. I wasn't prepared for how much it would change me.

The first change was personal and painful. Sylvia had had difficulty with my ambition. I valued both her and my marriage, but I couldn't have been myself if I remained satisfied with the status quo in my career. I wanted to climb as fast and as high as I could. This meant that more of my time and attention was being devoted to my work than to her. She was never demanding or unfair, and my inattention had nothing to do with my feelings for her. I simply wanted to succeed equally in my business career and in my marriage. In the beginning, I was confident that I could do both. By the time I accepted the opportunity in San Francisco, I realized that I couldn't. Sylvia was pleased for me and proud of me. But I went to San Francisco alone.

Watching my marriage dissolve was as upsetting to me as you might expect. I threw myself into my work and into adapting to my new life, which made my discomfort bearable.

I was working in the heart of one of the world's most interesting and exciting cities. All the famous locations that I had been hearing and reading about for much of my life—Fisherman's Wharf, the Golden Gate Bridge, Napa Valley, Yosemite Park—were just down the street or an hour or two away by car. But it was the lifestyle, both business and personal, that made the biggest impact on me. Toronto had had a classic northern WASP approach to work. Things there were done formally—men in three-piece suits (never leaving your own office without wearing the jacket), women in heels and dresses—and with a solemn approach to getting things done seven days a week, if necessary. In Toronto, I had bought into the idea completely, never leaving the office until the boss had gone home, and spending much of Saturdays and Sundays on projects. It wasn't quite like prison, but it smacked at least a little of military-style discipline.

If Toronto evoked life in the army, San Francisco suggested summer camp. Almost none of the men wore vests with their suits, everyone seemed to come and go as they pleased, and the idea of working on weekends unless totally necessary would be a form of sacrilege. Weekends were for sailing, hiking, jogging, or hanging out in Sausalito or Golden Gate Park, sampling music and art.

And everyone smiled! Work didn't seem to get anyone down. Life appeared to buoy them up. It was the relaxed atmosphere of San Francisco that first suggested to me the wisdom of trying to make work as enjoyable as play. For a businessman from Toronto, this was a revelation. For a kid from Sudbury, it was Disneyland, the beach, an extended recess and Saturday morning all rolled into one.

The most surprising discovery was that things were done well and on time, even if all day and every day was not devoted to work. In San Francisco it was possible—almost advised—to knock off each day at 6 PM, do no work at all on weekends, and still be productive. No deadlines were missed, and no hair was pulled out in frustration. Everyone seemed more efficient because their work and life were in better balance. In California I could get as much done as I had in Toronto and still have a social life.

All that Glitters... Is in L.A.

It took a while for me to adjust to the lifestyle, but eventually I did, and with great enthusiasm. I was pleased with my move, but I kept looking up the ladder at the next rung above me. In time, that rung was marked Office Head. My goal was to move beyond working on benefits communication alone, to take on more responsibility and deal with broader issues. I wanted to manage my own office, run my own show, choose and manage my own staff. I would seize the opportunity even if it meant giving up California, which I had come to love, in favor of a place like Denver. I had heard that the top job at the Denver office was coming available, and I began dropping hints about wanting to fill the position.

When my hints reached the ears of top management at Mercer, the word came back to me loud and rapidly. And also bluntly. I was informed that I likely would never run my own Mercer office. I was doing well at managing the communications side of things; that's where the top brass believed I belonged—and, I was told, that's where I should expect to stay. Which wasn't good enough for me. Within a few weeks I was offered the position of regional vice president of Mercer's rival, Johnson & Higgins, working out of Century City in Los Angeles, California. I didn't think twice.

LOS ANGELES WAS warmer and the traffic was worse, but I adapted to the city quickly. It took me longer to find my footing at Johnson & Higgins (J&H), which fostered a different environment from Mercer. At Mercer, things were down-to-earth and workmanlike. There may have been status levels within the hierarchy of the company—there always are—but people were more focused on achievements than on personal image. Where you came from or who you were seemed less important than what you could do, and how well you could do it. Things, I heard, were different at J&H, where image was valued, glitter was prized and whatever degree you had earned was less important than the college you attended to earn it.

Still, I was in Los Angeles. More than that, my office was in Century City, on the western fringe of Beverly Hills itself. Everywhere I looked I saw all the clichés that kids from the north—or people of any age from everywhere—had heard and seen about Southern California. There was the Hollywood sign on the hillside, and over to the west were the beaches of Santa Monica; even the name of the area our offices were in was reminiscent of Hollywood. When I stepped outside of our office building I was on the original set of 20th Century Fox, where some of the greatest movies in history had been made, and some of the biggest stars had strolled or arrived in their chauffeur-driven limousines.

I wasn't star-struck—just aware of my shiny new surroundings, and of my own success to that point. But I was struck by something else when a slim and tall blonde woman named Cayce Malone introduced herself to me at J&H. Cayce was the epitome of the term California girl. She was bright, funny, athletic and beautiful, and as aware as I was about the potential problems of combining work and personal relationships. I couldn't get her off my mind.

One day, I was driving to the airport on my way for a business trip. Cayce had come with me to drive my car back to the office. On the way, I blurted out the fact that she was on my mind far more than she should be. To my surprise and delight, she admitted that she had the same problem with me.

Okay, we broke a small guideline—but not really an ethical rule—about office romances. Neither of us was married or in any kind of relationship at the time. We soon became engaged, and were married in 1985. I have made many important decisions in my career, from leaping at an entry-level office job to seizing an opportunity to change companies and locations, without a second thought. But when it comes to wisdom and personal satisfaction, none exceeds my marriage to Cayce.

Where You Are Is More Important than Where You Came From

Before meeting Cayce, I had grown more aware of the status aspect at J&H. It appeared to me that an employee's background seemed to count as much as his or her ability. This was driven home in a casual hallway conversation I had with an actuary I'll call Fred. Actuaries are the people in insurance companies who plot the odds. Not the odds of winning a horse race or lottery. The odds of disasters, including automobile accidents, house fires, terrorist attacks, and how many people of a specific age group, gender, occupation and location—among other qualities—are likely to die in the next year. Or two. Or twenty. It's all about risk management, which is essential for insurance companies. For many actuaries, their professional perspective also cultivates something of a fatalistic view of life.

I had arrived at J&H a few months earlier, riding in on a wave of renown as the hot-shot guy who had almost single-handedly defined benefits communications, changing it from an industry ornament to a money-making, reputation-enhancing, marketing-advantage subsidy to company profits. If I thought this reputation cemented my front-runner position in the company, Fred made a point of bringing me down to earth by sharing his views with me.

"You know," Fred said with total sincerity, "you'll never get anywhere in this company unless you come out of USC, you're tall, you're good-looking, and you dress well." Fred, I should mention, was a short overweight guy who appeared to choose his wardrobe at Goodwill. I wasn't much taller than Fred, and instead of coming out of the University of Southern California, I had graduated from a Sudbury high school. I think I had a better sense of style than Fred, but that's not the point.

Fred was not top management material and he knew it, as did almost everyone else at J&H. Fred's bigger problem was that he assumed that some sort of decree existed to determine who achieved success in the company. Those guidelines, he believed, prevented him from rising to the level of success he knew he deserved, or at least one that he might covet. And it was all garbage.

I don't believe guidelines of any kind—the written or unwritten rules of business—should prevent anyone from realizing all the success that he or she is capable of achieving. Yes, there is prejudice in business, as there is everywhere in society. It's racial, gender-based and flows from a dozen other unfair points of view. It shouldn't exist, and it takes a number of skills to overcome it. The most important is probably determination. But that's not the kind of barrier Fred referred to. The biggest barrier Fred encountered was in his own mind.

I wanted to give Fred two bits of advice.

The first would be: *Never allow other people to shape your life for you*. This includes refusing to believe anyone who says your dreams are impossible or your abilities are limited. The only one who can seriously assess the combination of talent and ambition available for your success is you. Everyone else can go to hell.

The other piece of advice: *Identify any restrictions on your success and, if necessary, toss out those you can't change*. Not everyone can grasp that concept. Most of us are conditioned to find a way of working within the existing rules, even if it means compromising our deeply held convictions and our goals. Carving your own path while working within an established corporate milieu takes more than mere ambition. It takes courage.

The difference between ambition and courage is the difference between settling for mediocrity and demanding success. Ambition can take you where you know you want to go; courage takes you to heights you may never have dreamed of achieving. You get there the hard way, without shortcuts. There are no shortcuts to take you anywhere worth going. I acquired the roots of this attitude growing up in Sudbury, when I was determined to escape the mines, the abuse, the cold, and the inevitable path that others assumed their lives would follow.

These ideas had been percolating in my mind for some time, and hearing Fred speak of barriers and restrictions made me more aware of them. They didn't fully crystalize, however, until the day I watched live TV coverage of Julie Moss completing the 1982 Ironman Triathlon. In front of millions of viewers, she demonstrated what it takes to ignore restrictions and expectations, to stick to one's principles, and to achieve something that, in her case, extended beyond victory.

Inspiration from a Spectacular Collapse

The Ironman Triathlon is rightly considered the world's most difficult and challenging one-day sporting event. It begins with a 2.4-mile (3.86 km) swim in ocean water, followed by a 112-mile (180.25 km) bicycle race and a 26.22-mile (42.2 km) run, raced in that order, with no rest between the events. Participants who complete all three within seventeen hours are designated as Ironmen, regardless of gender.

No matter how athletic you are, taking part in the Ironman is a challenge of immense proportions. I was unaware of just how demanding the sport was until, sitting in an easy chair, I watched twenty-four-year-old Julie Moss run through the dying light of the day and approach the finish line in Kailua-Kona, Hawaii. In her senior year of college, she had been majoring in physical education and searching for a thesis subject. The Ironman seemed to fit—she would participate in the race intending to do her best, but the purpose was basically to obtain material for her thesis. It may have been primarily an academic endeavor, but Julie Moss had no intention of going through the motions. She gave every leg of the event her best. After swimming two and a half miles, pedaling her bicycle 112 miles and running twenty-six miles of the marathon, she was leading all other female competitors and approaching the finish line. That's when I tuned in the television coverage.

With other viewers numbering in the millions, I sat watching this slender young woman, dehydrated and in agony, collapse within a half-mile of the finish line. She rose and resumed running, only to fall again. And again. Each time she tried to stand—under the rules, none of the spectators could assist her—her legs gave out again. Over and over she tried to rise, then collapsed. While the crowd watched, some cheering and some weeping, she realized she could rise no more, and she crawled on the ground for the last twenty feet of the race.

Julie Moss finished second in the women's division. To those of us watching, she won without doubt. I had never seen anyone with the grit and determination Julie Moss showed that day, and I have not seen anyone match it since.

I hadn't been familiar with the Ironman until then. To me, it seemed impossible for any human being to complete the race in the seventeen-hour maximum time limit. Yet many did. I wanted to try, even though I faced a major hurdle from the very beginning: I couldn't swim. Still, I couldn't stop thinking about attempting something that everyone—including me—would deem impossible to do. I made up my mind to take part in the Ironman the following year, and began training for it.*

The initial step, of course, would be to take swimming lessons. That sounds easy, but it wasn't. After watching my attempts in the water, the first two swimming coaches I went to believed I couldn't do anything except imitate an anchor. I finally located one who promised to teach me how to swim two and a half miles in the ocean in under two hours and fifteen minutes. I wouldn't challenge any Olympic records, but I was unlikely to drown in the process.

The next leg was bicycling, and this I could do well. I loved the cycling stage of the Ironman, and spent as much time as I could spare from the swimming lessons perfecting my ability on two wheels. The last stage of running a marathon was a major test in itself, but I was already a good runner, and I worked on improving both my speed and endurance.

The Ironman requires American competitors to qualify each year. I had no chance of qualifying for the 1983 competition, but entrants from other countries could bypass the qualification. One of my brothers lived in Saskatchewan, so I used his address on my application, and in October 1983 I lined up with about 1,500 other competitors, waiting for the sound of the starter's gun to dive into the water.

I barely managed to finish the swim portion within the qualifying time, but once on my bike I passed a large number of riders over the 112-mile course. Off the bike and in the run I did even better, outpacing half the field on the way to the finish line.

I didn't win, but I completed the event in about thirteen hours, which put me in Julie Moss's league. I achieved something that once had seemed impossible to me. I had moved off the sofa where I had watched Julie refuse to give up under agonizing conditions, and competed in the same event a year later. Not bad for a guy well into his

* I have since learned that many people contacted Julie to say that watching her finish the 1982 Ironman inspired them to train and participate in various events, from half-marathons to the Ironman itself. This, despite the fact that she hadn't won the race. It wasn't winning the race that was important in the end. It was her refusal to fail by insisting on finishing with what often appeared to be her last breath.

thirties. I completed the next Hawaiian Ironman competition in 1984, and finished the Ironman in New Zealand a year later in 1985, improving my times with each race.

So what, you may be asking, does this have to do with business ethics and Donald Trump?

The Sad Folly of Cheating

Let's be up-front here: Business is hardly the only activity in America, and elsewhere, that suffers from a widespread lack of integrity. My focus on it in this book is the result of many factors, beginning with the reality that the current occupant of the White House has displayed an appalling lack of integrity in his business dealings and his personal life. I worry that the influence of Donald Trump, filling the highest office of the land, will be disastrous if his actions represent a standard for conducting business, addressing racial and gender concerns, and a host of other measures. I feel I can also speak on the subject with some authority because, like countless other entrepreneurs in the United States, I launched and managed a business built on ethical values.

No activity, including both amateur and professional sports, is immune to Trump's style of ensuring personal victory. What we see and learn from the goings-on in the athletic arena can serve as a cautionary tale for how bad things become if principles are casually discarded anywhere in society.

Enough examples of cheating in sporting events have been discovered in recent years to suggest that it is more widespread than we may ever know... and that the heroes many of us admire may be worthy of our contempt and nothing more.

I suppose no one epitomizes cheating in sports more than bicyclist Lance Armstrong. It's not just the scope of his deceit—winning seven Tour de France titles, thanks to the use of performance-enhancing drugs, and pocketing more than $200 million in prize money, endorsements and other earnings.[38] It's the audacity he displayed while doing it that's even more disillusioning, threatening lawsuits against anyone who dared suggest that Armstrong was a cheat and a liar. Of course, he was both of these.

The motive for cheating in sports can be akin to the goal behind cheating in business. Participants in both are driven by greed, by the chance of earning maximum levels of income with minimum effort. But not all are motivated by money alone. At the outset they seek glory, publicity and honor, sometimes by the most blatant means. No one in my memory was more brazen in her tactics than Rosie Ruiz, who claimed to have won the 1980 Boston Marathon in record time. Crowned the winner in the women's category, it was later discovered that much of her "run" had been made by subway. Ruiz stepped off the subway car and burst through a group of spectators half a mile from the finish line. Rosie sought praise and respect. Instead, her name is associated with rebuke and disgrace.

But does cheating in sports really matter? Sports, after all, are a diversion, something to pass the time and entertain us. Fans may denounce cheating, but in the end, it has little impact on the "real" world—the one in which we work and raise our families. But cheating, as I noted, isn't limited to sports. It's an option open to anyone prepared to do what it takes to seize a prize—money, fame, or whatever. To people who choose cheating in any aspect of the game of life, qualities such as honesty, integrity and fairness have no value.

So it does matter. It matters well beyond the racetrack, the ice rink, the baseball diamond and the tennis courts. Because if our sports heroes are exposed as cheaters, doesn't that lower the bar for the rest of us? If it's okay for our role models and celebrities, is it okay for us? Do we become immune to the idea of cheating when we see it all around us, and it's passed off as acceptable behavior? Sporting championships that are won fair and square are decided according to the same principles required to succeed legitimately and in a principled way in business. Determination, energy, effort, teamwork, planning and a host of other qualities are as key in business as they are in sports. But the other cyclists who watched Lance Armstrong steal victories and money from them in his multiple wins over the years saw all their work made worthless by someone who refused to understand the value of ethics.

We don't need Rosie Ruizs or Lance Armstrongs in American business. Cheating in the boardroom is as disgraceful as cheating on the racetrack. Every illegal shortcut to score new highs in sales and profit says that you don't really have to work hard, you don't need to sacrifice, you don't need to respect yourself or your customers or your competitors or even your own employees to succeed. You just need to be prepared to break laws and regulations, to lie and conceal. It advises everyone else in your industry or profession to throw away their concept of values and do whatever they can get away with. That's not the way I want to do business. It is certainly not the way I want our politicians to behave either. But we have seen this kind of behavior become almost the norm in both spheres.

Since I no longer have a business to manage, I am past being directly concerned about the ethics of those I employ and with whom I deal. I remain deeply concerned, however, about business ethics generally and the impact they have on what it means to be an American. *Ethics and principles matter*. They matter in sports, in business, in personal relationships and in every other aspect of society. As a grandparent, my perspective has become more sharply focused on the world my children and grandchildren will occupy. I do not want it to be a world in which anything goes. I don't want them to buy into the comment of an NFL coach who, when caught breaking the rules, defended his actions by claiming, "If you're not cheating, you're not trying hard enough." (The line has since been attributed to various sports figures.)

The world I value and admire is the one that Julie Moss inhabits, the one in which she refused to give up. She insisted on competing according to rules that applied to everyone else. When spectators, stricken by her suffering and her dilemma, tried to assist her, to lift her to her feet and walk her to the finish line, she waved them off. That wasn't the way things were done. She would do it the way everyone else in the race was expected to finish—fair and square and on the very little steam remaining in mind and body. She finished the race the hard way, and earned admiration and respect from everyone familiar with her experience, showing that fair competition is often not easy, but the result is more meaningful, more fulfilling and legitimately won.

There are no degrees of honesty. There is no middle ground between fairness and fraud. And there is no future for a society that assumes that the only way to win at any endeavor is to dispense with rules and display no respect for the rights and expectations of others. If we do not insist on ethics in business, how can we demand it anywhere else?

By the way, whenever I mention the incredible feat of Julie Moss, someone invariably shares my memory of, and enthusiasm for, her courage and insistence on finishing the race on her own, followed by expressions of admiration for her personal heroism. No one can recall who won the women's portion of the event, as well-deserved as it was. Julie's accomplishment overshadowed it. Now there's a lesson for those who seek glory and praise in competition.

No One Needed to Defend Me

There are many ways to build a reputation in a business or profession. The most obvious is to work hard and be damn good at what you do. I managed to do that from my first day on the job, filing documents at Manulife in Sudbury. I also acted with honesty and integrity in everything I did. Whatever the guideline, I played by the rules.

One of the key rules in any business is the need to maintain honest records, which was a problem at J&H. Computerized accounting programs were just coming into vogue, and they permitted some practical steps to be taken easily. One of these was tracking work that had been completed but had yet to be billed. Many of the projects my team and I worked on would extend for months, but interim billing was not permitted under the terms of the contract. I began to apply TBR (To Be Reversed) invoices listing the amount of income we had generated to date on the books. The invoice was completed with everyone's knowledge, but never issued. On the contracted completion date all TBR invoices were deleted and replaced with the final invoice forwarded to the client. It was an effective means of tracking my department's productivity, but somehow the accountants at J&H couldn't grasp the idea. Each time they queried the step, I would patiently explain the process to them over and over.

On the day after I returned from New Zealand, having finished my third Ironman Triathlon, my manager complained about the process yet again. I reminded him of how it worked, the role it played in tracking my department's success, and how widely it was being applied in other companies and other industries.

He still didn't get it. Or maybe he didn't want to. "Damn it!" he barked at me, "I'm getting tired of defending you to everybody!" But I had done nothing wrong, and I deeply resented his suggestion that I had. Whether it was my self-confidence from completing another Ironman or simply a build-up of frustration from working with a company that couldn't seem to keep up with technology, his words were all the impetus I needed to strike out on my own. The idea arrived like a lightning bolt.

Oh, the thought of forming my own company had skipped through my mind now and then, as I'm sure it does with all ambitious businesspeople. But in that moment, everything crystalized. If someone was going to question my scruples when they had no reason to, if they were going to call my reputation into question for no reason, I wasn't going to stand for it. I had toyed with the idea of starting a company I could put my own stamp on, where I could live by my principles and expect the same of those who worked with me. At the time, this back-handed accusation about my business practices was the catalyst I needed. "There is no better moment for me to go," I told myself. Within a week, I was gone.

One member of my staff came with me. I had no money, no clients and no office. Everything became a gamble that I was prepared to take. I cashed in my 401(k) to buy computers and furniture, established an office in our small house in West Hollywood, and went to work.

Yes, there were bumps. And disappointments. And sweaty nights worrying about making payrolls and building the business and choosing the right staff. But I got to run a business the way I thought it should be run, to live and work according to my standards and principles, and I loved every minute of it.

11

Deeds, Not Words (2)

MY DECISION TO leave the security of J&H and launch my own company may suggest I was taking a big gamble. In some ways I suppose it was—a leap from the safe arms of "the corp" to building a business on my own. But like all dedicated entrepreneurs, armed with both the skills and the determination to succeed on their own, I never felt like I was rolling the dice on my future. I felt secure in the knowledge that I would succeed, and that much of my future success would stem from the reputation I had built over the years.

I don't pretend to be the most brilliant individual who ever worked in communications. But I do take a lot of comfort in the knowledge that, over the years with two giant international employers, I had sought to treat both my clients and my coworkers fairly. Bad news travels fast, I believe, but good news carries more weight. Get caught cheating on a client or your employer, or being unfair to a staff member or subordinate, and the news is likely to travel at the speed of sound. Maintain full honesty in your dealings and meet every promise you make, and it may not generate the legendary conversation at the water cooler (these days it's more like a chat over a latte), but with time, a foundation of trust is built.

Thanks to the reputation I took with me when I left to form Sheppard Associates, I managed to build a raft of good clients within a few years. There were crises along the way, of course—nights when I would worry if my accounts receivable would exceed my accounts payable, and days when I wondered if we would win a competition for a new client. In time, we prospered. Cayce and I grew confident enough to start a family and purchase a large house in an affluent suburb where we could enjoy security and the rewards of hard work and dedication.

Our world had changed for the better. The world for many others, however, remained challenging and desperate. Before dawn on an October morning in 1999, these two worlds collided when I stepped out of the heaven that was my home with my family, and into a temporary and frightening hell. In a word, I was mugged.

It was just after 5 AM and I was about to leave for the airport on (what else?) a business trip. I stepped out the front door of our home in La Cañada Flintridge, carrying my laptop computer and briefcase. Inside the briefcase was my cell phone and cash. I was about to place the computer and briefcase in my car when four men appeared out of the hedges where they had been hiding. In the glow of the streetlamp I could see that at least one of them was armed.

Everyone, I suppose, has a definition of courage and bravery. I'm not sure what mine was, but there was no way I would let these guys get into my home, where Cayce and our two young children were sleeping. I ignored the gun—maybe courage is linked at least a little to insanity—and began fighting back, screaming in the loudest voice I could muster. About all my screams seemed to attract was a pistol-whipping, with punches and kicks added to the mix. Finally, one of them grabbed my laptop and briefcase and ran down the road with them. He was followed by his buddies who, I assume, were worried that my shouts would bring the police.

The police soon arrived, joined by paramedics who dealt with some cuts over my eye and on the back of my head. I don't know why the muggers didn't fire their weapons. I didn't care either, of course. I was just glad to return to Cayce and our children, forgetting about the business trip and adding the incident to my list of life's adventures.

According to the police, the attack had been planned and I had been the target from the beginning. This did not make me feel better.

Flattening the Playing Field, One Kid at a Time

You never forget an experience like that. Those kinds of traumatic events, I suspect, change everyone who encounters them in ways that they may not realize at the time. My first reaction, of course, was anger—not just at the actions of those thugs but at the risk they represented to my family. They had wanted me to let them into my home, something I was prepared to prevent with my life. And while I refused to totally forgive them, I suspect that something happened within me to change my outlook at least a little.

I had some idea about what makes anyone become violently aggressive toward another person who is better off than they are. We lived in an upscale neighborhood, I was a successful businessperson, my laptop and briefcase identified me as a likely target, and the muggers had a need to fill—maybe it was for drugs, for food, for their own pride; who knows? My biggest fear was that my children might have been taken and held for ransom.

This excuses nothing on the part of the muggers. But as time passed, I found myself growing aware of others in less-attractive corners of Los Angeles, understanding their plight and feelings of helplessness. The kid from Sudbury—the one who grew up in the shack without running water, wearing threadbare hand-me-down clothes and itching to find a better life for himself—still roamed around inside my head. As a child, I had no one to reach a helping hand to me. But maybe I could offer one to kids in similar situations. Perhaps I could perform some deed that would give me satisfaction but, more important, would benefit kids in a manner that might similarly have benefited me if someone had paid attention to my needs as an underprivileged child. And I did.

Like so many good things, it began at home. Our eight-year-old son, Malone, took an interest in soccer. When our daughter had played soccer in a girl's league I had been involved, eventually becoming a divisional soccer coach. I grew to appreciate the game. Talk about baseball, football, hockey and basketball all you want, but soccer remains the truly universal sport, "the beautiful game" that is played and enjoyed everywhere in the world. All you need is a soccer ball, a reasonably flat field, a few players and you practically have a match.

The biggest recreational soccer program in the country is the American Youth Soccer Organization (AYSO). More than half a million kids, from four to eighteen years old, play soccer in the AYSO, and it seemed like a good place for my son to get a taste of the sport and have some fun.

When I took Malone to register in AYSO, I noticed a predominance of white middle-class kids signing up with their parents, despite the fact that a substantial number of Hispanic families lived in the area covered by our local AYSO chapter. While I wondered about this, a Hispanic woman arrived and asked to register her two boys in the program. When she was told the registration fee was $100 per child, her face fell.

The $100, I knew, covered a lot of things. The fee bought a uniform and an entire season's play for each child, but a hundred bucks was beyond the reach of most Hispanic families. The guy registering the players on this day was a friend of mine. I handed him two hundred dollars to have the two boys registered. Then I turned to Maria and told her that if she knew any other families who wanted to register their children for soccer but needed help, I would cover the cost. "Please don't advertise it," I said. "I just want to help kids play soccer."

She gave me the names of deserving families who loved the idea of their children participating in soccer but the fee was out of reach for them. By the time the registration period was finished, about twenty Hispanic kids played soccer that season—wearing their AYSO uniforms, running across the grass, getting exercise, having fun. It just might have been the best $2,000 investment I made that year.

It made me feel good about myself. I was able to assist others, thanks to my success in business. But something was missing. The policy of AYSO was to have fun. In fact, one of their key rules required every club to put every player in the game at least once during a match. They called it fair play. It was great for participation, but it didn't do much for competition. And I love competition.

I enjoyed working with AYSO but if I were to become deeply involved in the game it had to be somewhere that supported the urge to compete—to celebrate the joy of winning and deal with the disappointment of losing. AYSO gave trophies just for participating in the game, so that no one had their feelings hurt. That's heart-warming but it's recreational soccer, not reality. Reality tells us that we encounter failures as well as victories, and if we are smart and aware we learn from our failures. Reality means competition, and I wanted to support that concept.

I did it by dedicating time, money, energy along with volumes of blood, sweat and tears into building a club soccer organization in the Los Angeles area. Club soccer was about kids having fun, just like AYSO. But it was also about encouraging serious competition between teams and leagues, supporting and expanding the pool of gifted soccer players who one day could help the United States become a serious opponent in world-class competition. It was the only route to professional world-class status, and without it, the sport would never achieve the prominence it deserved in America.* At the time, playing soccer with the ambition of participating in a World Cup championship was an almost hopeless objective for many American kids. Those hoping to gain a college scholarship for their soccer skills needed to be rated at the highest levels of club soccer, because that's where college recruiters scouted and selected candidates. And many of the disadvantaged and minority families I was trying to help could never afford to go that route.

Club soccer in the United States is a pay-to-play sport. If you or your children want to participate in this competitive arena, it will cost you perhaps a couple of thousand dollars per season to cover the cost of professional coaches, equipment, travel and tournament fees.

* Of course, elsewhere in the world the sport is known as football, in various translations—*futbol* in Spanish, *Fußball* in German, and so on. With an American audience in mind, I'll stick to *soccer*.

Soccer training is virtually year-round and, with scant support from sponsors, it's up to the families of young soccer players to pull out their credit cards and checkbooks at the start of every season. Many families cannot possibly afford to invest that kind of money in their kids' sports activities. The solution was for someone to create a club soccer team in which disadvantaged kids and minorities would be both encouraged and enabled to participate, and the key was to eliminate the pay-to-play aspect. The "someone," I knew, was me. If they couldn't get access to club soccer, I would bring it to them.

I created the Arroyo United Soccer Club, applying for membership in the Coast Soccer League. We needed a shorter, more memorable name for the team itself, and we came up with The Flyers. I began visiting soccer clubs in Europe and Mexico, searching for proven ways of discovering and grooming youngsters with outstanding potential. There was no conflict in my mind between providing the opportunity to have fun playing soccer as well as the chance to develop their skills to the optimum level. Club soccer was the way to achieve both.

My focus remained on assisting minorities to participate in the game, at an organized level. So in a gesture that meant a great deal to Latino families in the area, I changed the name of the club from the Flyers to the Los Angeles Football Club or, as it's more commonly referred to by fans, the LAFC. For many families, of course, it would take more than a new name to help their kids participate. So the membership fees were structured to subsidize the cost for a fixed number of families; a cushion was built into the full fees charged to those families who could afford them, and I would make up any deficits that might accrue.

Let's be clear: I was still the aggressive tough-but-fair business guy who had climbed out of a mining culture and built a chain of busy service offices across the United States. I wasn't encouraging people to sing "Kumbaya" and toss rose petals in the air; I simply recognized an unfair situation that deserved attention from someone who gave a damn. It just seemed like the decent thing for a guy like me to do. How can you claim to have values and close your eyes to injustices that you know exist and that you can help correct? This has nothing to do with political views and everything to do with personal integrity—the awareness that life consists of more than making enough money to purchase diamond cufflinks for your custom-made shirts and solid-gold faucets for your bathtub.

I had seen the way poverty and prejudice affected so many kids in L.A. I knew the pleasure and satisfaction they would earn from participating in a sport they could enjoy. And I had both the energy and wherewithal to make it happen. Why wouldn't I do what I could to help fulfill their dreams? It was the decent thing to do.

My efforts to promote and support competitive soccer in the Los Angeles area included arranging a match between two celebrated European teams, Chelsea and Inter Milan, in the Rose Bowl. All proceeds would be used to expand the opportunities for underprivileged kids to play in the LAFC. The event generated enormous coverage, including a feature in the *New York Times*.[39]

More than eighty thousand people filled the Rose Bowl, enough to convince me I was doing something worthwhile, something of value to those beyond my own family and circle of friends. I went on to promote package trips to the World Cup in South Africa the following year, seek an arrangement with the New York Cosmos professional soccer team, and engage much of the U.S. soccer establishment—all in the interests of finding ways for underprivileged boys and girls to engage in a game they loved.

Not everything worked. And the things that didn't work—and that I had agreed to underwrite—deflated my bank account substantially. The cost in cash and time put a strain on my family life. The entire process was further complicated with various twists and turns, most of them the result of less-than-scrupulous people more interested in lining their own pockets than in helping to promote soccer and assist underprivileged kids and their families. I had achieved much, however. An untold number of kids who might never have had the chance to play competitive soccer and enjoy all the fun and health benefits had participated in the world's favorite sport.

I had done my part and it was time to move on. So I walked away from soccer. And hopped on a bicycle.

12

"How're You Doin' Now, Sucker?"

TURNING SIXTY-FIVE YEARS of age marks a dramatic point in life. Many people are programmed to declare themselves retired, and settle down to a future of playing bridge, socializing, and either feeling free of their working career or lamenting its passing.

Approaching my sixty-fifth birthday, I felt blessed. I had a wonderful warm marriage, a terrific family, and a reasonably large asset base earned through almost fifty years of hard work. Along with all of these benefits, and perhaps the most important of all, I was in reasonably good health.

I say "reasonably" because, while I had participated in marathons and triathlons over the previous twenty-five years, I had become less active with time. But I suffered no serious health problems. My heart was strong, and the rest of my body functioned at the level you might expect for a man halfway through his seventh decade.

I also was unconcerned about "retiring," whatever that meant. I had sold my company some years earlier and spent the intervening years enjoying my family and building the opportunity for kids to play competitive soccer. Who needed "retirement"? Still, reaching age sixty-five is a milestone of sorts and I decided to mark it somehow.

The idea was appealing. I could challenge myself in new ways. All I had to do was make a decision. Should I go back to school, perhaps to earn a university degree? Start a new business? Find a hobby? See the world? Meanwhile, I sat around gaining weight and sensing my brain cells wandering off to enjoy permanent siestas. Then the notion struck me: why not find a way to get my body in better physical condition while continuing to help underprivileged kids, even in places beyond Southern California—like Africa? And the insane, impractical and irresistible answer followed: ride a bicycle across America, Pacific to Atlantic, with supporters pledging contributions for every mile along the way! My swimming skills still were far from Olympic caliber, and running for days on end would be slow and boring. But I had always loved cycling. Spending six weeks on two wheels bent over a pair of handlebars may not appeal to everyone, but it sounded ideal to me.

I spent more than a year planning, organizing and shaping up for the journey. I would ride from Santa Barbara to Charleston, South Carolina, taking forty-one days to travel the 3,215 miles through (I hoped) mild and pleasant autumn air. The more I thought about the ride, the more excited I became. It would be a romantic adventure, tracing the routes of secondary roads, seeing Middle America and meeting people who shared my values and dreams for the country. Most of all it would test my strength, both physical and mental, and raise significant funds for worthy causes.

To help me focus on rising each day to face from 35 to 140 miles of pedaling, I relied on a company called Trek Travel. They provided guides, arranged for accommodations each night, provided healthy energy-packed meals and (oh my!) a masseuse to relieve my muscle aches.

Still, I faced serious challenges along the way, made more severe by the fact that I was much older than most people who would tackle such a trip. And "romantic"? There was nothing romantic about encountering hail and freezing rain at 10,500 feet while climbing the Tusas Mountains dressed in light summer-weight clothing. Nor riding into headwinds on terrible roads with no shoulders, hoping the semis roaring past at sixty-five miles per hour remembered to leave room for me. From time to time I was physically attacked by dogs that saw me either as a threat to their dominance or as a passing porterhouse steak, and threatened by angry commuters who flew into a rage because it took them an extra few seconds to get past my guides and me.

At times like those, Reality pushed Romantic aside and growled in my ear, "How're you doin' now, sucker?" At other times I was doing fine. Especially when I remembered the bigger reason for riding, which had less to do with my fitness and pride and more to do with the people I wanted to benefit from the journey.

I was pursuing the same motive that had steered me into working on behalf of underprivileged kids who wanted to play soccer. I don't believe in being selective about personal integrity; we have an obligation to help those who need our assistance in various spheres of our life. First, we all have needs to fulfill for ourselves and our families. Some are basic, like paying the rent or mortgage and putting food on the table. Others add to our comfort and general enjoyment of life. When all of these needs are satisfied, we have the pleasurable option of looking around to see what we can do for others.

I chose three charities to receive the proceeds: Young Life Capernaum, which provides adventures for children with disabilities; Project GOAL, an educational nonprofit organization supporting athletes; and the Women's Institute for Secondary Education and Research (WISER), of which I'll speak more later.

Looking back from the vantage point of today, the trip seems like something between a dream and an adventure movie. I have little recollection of the pain, the fatigue and the fear I felt over those six weeks. I recall clearly, however, the stunning beauty of the land (Tennessee was the most beautiful state) broken now and then by the tragic sight of boarded towns, abandoned houses and crumbling bridges. We live in a complex land set among both hope and despair.

My most deeply etched memory is from the final day, riding into Charleston with a police escort, an entire lane dedicated to our troupe. Seven miles from the shore and the end of the journey I received a video, via e-mail, from my daughter, Morgan, a touching tribute that turned on the waterworks. While I'm drying my eyes over it a voice behind me says "Hello there," and I turn to see my eldest sister, Shirley. She, along with her two sons and their partners, had driven nineteen hours nonstop from Sault Ste. Marie, Ontario, to meet me, all of it coordinated by Cayce. Had my heart not been so strong, I would have had an attack right there.

We resumed riding, leading a small parade to the Atlantic shore, where I dipped my bike in the ocean and reveled in the love around me and the pride within me. Back home I dispensed the checks for $66,618 and looked around for the next challenge to tackle during my retirement.

"Retirement"? You mean fishing or golfing or reading or...?

Not for me. Never for me.

Into Africa...with Soccer Balls

As I mentioned, the charities to receive donations from my ride across America included WISER, the Women's Institute for Secondary Education and Research. While I had been busy working to build and manage the LAFC, I learned about WISER through my daughter's attendance at Duke University. Dr. Sherryl Broverman, a biology professor at Duke, had been instrumental in launching the program, collaborating with Egerton University in Kenya.

Dr. Broverman had focused her group's efforts on helping girls and young women in the region of Muhuru Bay on the shore of Lake Victoria in Kenya. Young women and girls in that part of the world face every kind of challenge you can imagine, far more than the boys and men. They routinely dealt with extreme poverty, sexual exploitation, poor educational opportunities, high incidences of early pregnancies and extensive HIV infection. Many girls engaged in sexual activity with fishermen, laborers and their male teachers in return for food or passing marks. Add to this a lack of modern amenities such as electricity and fresh water, and it's easy to understand how the lives of most of these young women look both gloomy and preordained. For a very long time, women in the area have endured a cycle of early marriage, HIV and crushing poverty. In contrast, boys enjoy at least the prospect of a higher education and opportunities within and beyond the region.

Dr. Broverman led the way in establishing a private boarding school where girls could concentrate on nutrition and education and not be led down a path to pregnancy and diseases. When my daughter Morgan encountered Dr. Broverman and the WISER program, she was so impressed with all that they were achieving, and so enthusiastic about contributing to its success, that I decided to look into it on my own.

Similar efforts are in place throughout much of Africa and the Third World, and I silently applauded everything that WISER stood for. But when I learned that more than 96 percent of the graduates of the boarding school at Muhuru went on to university, I was more than impressed—I was motivated to help make a difference.

The first step in supporting efforts like WISER is easy, if you have both ample resources and sufficient concern. All you do is write a check or two. I did, for a few hundred thousand dollars. The suffering of the bright young women in the area touched my heart. It was all so unfair, so outrageous to me. Morgan, I knew, would never face nearly the number of injustices and inhumane ordeals in her life that the young women of Muhuru faced each day.

Money, of course, was just the beginning. The young women also needed a sense of empowerment, a promise that they and the daughters they may have in the future would no longer be at the mercy of both exploitive men and unsanitary conditions.

My support of WISER blossomed into a level of involvement and dedication that surprised everyone, including me. It began with my hands-on contribution to building the school for the girls, along with a badly needed water filtration plant. An investment of money and hard work, including battling with local contractors to do the job well and on time, meant that the young women of Muhuru would have a school to attend, a roof over their heads, beds to sleep in, fresh water to drink and the promise of a better life, which so many of us in America take for granted.

It didn't stop with education. Led by Dr. Broverman, WISER went beyond promoting the girls' education to helping older women realize their skills as entrepreneurs. Soon the women of Muhuru were trading cattle and launching businesses to provide income for their families, and independence and satisfaction for themselves. Almost overnight, it seemed, a reservoir of talent and ability was tapped. The women seized the chances with enthusiasm, growing successful businesses and supporting themselves and their families.

The results were measured in many ways. For myself, I recall seeing a group of young women who attended the school walking along a road, laughing in the sunshine, singing and playing, knowing they had a future they could look forward to instead of fearing. The promise of education, together with their faith, family and community, created smiles that, in their own way, were as warm and bright as the sun.

The other dimension to their lives that intrigued me was—no surprise—athletics. Girls need the fun and fitness benefits of competitive sports every bit as much as boys, and while boys in Muhuru always seemed to find a ball and a pitch for a football match after school, girls enjoyed no similar opportunity.

This was right up my alley. I arrived back in Muhuru the following year ready not just to build a soccer pitch but to introduce competitive girls' soccer, bringing about one hundred soccer balls and a pair of cleats for every girl enrolled at the school.

Out of this came, I believe, a major advance for the young women of Muhuru. And a lesson in life for me.

Lessons on Life in an African Village for "The Chelsea Man"

In Africa I wore a Chelsea jersey acquired when I organized the match between that team and Inter Milan in the Rose Bowl. So everywhere in Muhuru, I became known as "The Chelsea Man," the old white guy busy with WISER, helping the girls in the boarding school play soccer.

One day I was approached by a lovely young boy who introduced himself to me as Robert. He knew of my contributions to the girls' school and asked if he could have a soccer ball. I said, "Of course," and handed one to him. I took delight at the smile on his face when he thanked me for the ball and tore off back to his village to share the treasure with his friends.

I took no delight a few hours later when Sherryl Broverman tracked me down and asked if it was true that I had given a soccer ball to one of the boys in the village. I replied that indeed I had, and was about to explain my generosity when Sherryl straightened me out.

The entire community, she pointed out, knew that I had given Robert the soccer ball. Which meant to them, with perfect logic, that others could claim a free soccer ball as well, and we could expect them all to appear, asking for a soccer ball like the one Robert received. "You can't do that," she reminded me. "You don't have enough soccer balls for everyone. So what did you just do?" I had made myself feel good, she suggested, by giving a ball to Robert. But in fact, the gesture was not helpful to anyone—it was destructive to the entire program. "That is not the way you build a community," Sherryl explained. "And that's what we're trying to do here—build a community."

She was correct, of course. No one would have thought less of me for telling Robert that I was sorry but the soccer balls were intended for use by the girls in the school only.

The bigger lesson was one I had learned during my years in business but had ignored amid the joy and satisfaction of helping out in Muhuru. Like leadership, doing good sometimes means saying no. You can't always be a hero—not if it involves a decision that, in the long run, proves destructive. I would love to have seen every child in the region with his or her own soccer ball, but that's not what I was there for. I was there to help the girls and young women rise up out of abuse and hopelessness through education, pride, security and trust to realize all of their potential. Achieving this goal involved many things, including access to clean water and the opportunity to enjoy competitive sports. It did not involve causing serious disruption in all our efforts just to enjoy a young man's smile of gratitude.

None of this changed my delight at seeing the impact of WISER on the girls of Muhuru and the community generally. Nor did it shake my conviction that those of us who have achieved great material goals in our lives can find few more satisfying things to do with the rest of the time we are given on earth than to share both—our time and our wealth—with others. It's the decent thing to do.

PART THREE

Take It from the Top: The Fundamental Role of Values-Based Leadership

13

Who Matters Most?

IF TALK IS cheap, lip service is a bargain.

Far too many business leaders and organizations pay lip service to the idea of ethics. Few of them dare to publicly suggest that American business cannot choose to do anything it pleases in the pursuit of profit. Everywhere in business, just as everywhere else in American society, standards of principled behavior should apply. Too often we encounter actions that would never be tolerated between private citizens but that some business executives believe are appropriate. No one is likely to forget, for a very long time, the sight of a passenger being dragged down the aisle of the United Airlines aircraft, his face bloodied and screaming in pain and outrage. The man sincerely believed that, having paid for the seat and settling himself into it, he had a right not to be arbitrarily removed.

United had a different view. Yes, management agreed, the passenger had paid for the trip and was quietly awaiting takeoff. He had done nothing to qualify for ejection from the aircraft. Nor was he removed for safety reasons. It's just that United needed that seat for a crewmember to occupy. The crewmember, you see, would be needed to work on a flight leaving the destination. Could he or she have been sent on a flight with a competing airline? Apparently not. Might it be better for United not to overbook its flights, which it routinely does just to avoid flying an empty seat or two from time to time? This did not appear to be an option either. Both choices, you see, would affect United's profits.

Any time a publicly traded company puffs up its corporate chest and hangs a difficult decision on its bottom line, it effectively strokes the ego and anxiety of one exclusive group of people: its shareholders. Every act by a corporation, many business leaders argue, must be assessed in the interests of the company's shareholders. In that view, shareholders are a strange blend of touchstones, criteria, magistrates and infants. Their interests must be sacrosanct, their well-being satisfied and their disapproval avoided—sometimes to the detriment of other stakeholders.

Really?

At its heart, that's the very attitude that results in events such as the notorious eviction of the United passenger. Which, in turn, led to extensive shareholder revulsion, not their approval. Unhappy shareholders vote by shouting or entering "Sell!" into their telephones and computers. The day after the story of the evicted passenger broke around the world, United's share price fell 4.4 percent, wiping about $1 billion from the books. The stock recovered somewhat in the days immediately following the event, but the number of potential passengers who may reconsider United as their first-choice airline remains incalculable.*

The United fiasco resulted from a number of errors, but two override all others.

The first was to permit a relatively small concern about corporate expenses and bottom-line performance to prevail over basic ethical behavior. The second was to assume that a corporation's primary obligation when evaluating business decisions is to its shareholders. It is not.

* The impact was especially felt in China, where it was suspected that the passenger, who was of Asian descent, might have been chosen on ethnic/racial grounds. There is no evidence that this was the case.

This may sound like heresy to many people. Don't shareholders own the company? Don't their needs and concerns supersede those of every other group? Yes and no.

Yes, shareholders legally "own" a corporation, but unless they are actively involved in the business as managers or employers, they contribute almost nothing to the firm's actual operations. In fact, the vast majority of retail shareholders rarely choose to exercise their right to vote for or against corporate actions and policies. One 2015 report found that investors exercised their proxy votes to represent just 28 percent of outstanding shares they owned, leaving an estimated 97 billion retail shares unrepresented.[40] When they find themselves embarrassed by "their" company's behavior, however, many of the same shareholders dispense with the shares rather quickly.

Let's be blunt: Shareholders contribute money to a company's operations and success, and nothing else. Is the money important? Of course it is. But of all the things a publicly traded company requires to succeed, money is by far the most interchangeable. A dollar from a retiree in Idaho is basically the same as a dollar from a mutual fund in Chicago. Does one qualify for treatment different from the other? Certainly not legally. And absolutely not ethically.

Shareholders, for the most part, are free to walk away from their participation in corporate activities. They may have made money on their investment, in which case they walk away with profits. They may also, it's true, have lost money, so they walk away with experience. Either way, they can choose to leave whenever it is most convenient or profitable.

Those opportunities rarely exist for the other four major stakeholder groups involved in the activities of a publicly traded business: employees, customers, vendors and members of any community associated with the company. Their connections are more difficult to sever with a simple order to sell, and they can suffer more serious damage as a result of a company's misbehavior. They are also generally far more involved in the everyday life of the organization and far more influential, in many ways, on the company's success or failure. Almost every action by shareholders is either passive or occurs in the background of a company's operations. Compare that with the actions of employees who are involved forty or more hours each week; or suppliers, who anticipate and provide the products and services that keep the company functioning; or the communities that provide the infrastructure and essential services; or the customers, whose patronage and money represent the ultimate measure of a company's success or failure.

It all rather diminishes the importance of shareholders, doesn't it?

Who Is Ultimately Responsible for Ethical Behavior? We Are.

So when it comes to determining who most deserves acceptable ethical responsibilities from a business, how do we determine the involved groups that most deserve it? Here's my measure: *Ethical responsibility is owed to the individuals and groups most responsible for the company's success.*

Of the five groups mentioned earlier—employees, customers, vendors, communities and shareholders—surely it's clear that, while shareholders contribute to a company's existence, their contributions to its success may well be minimal compared to the others.

This flies in the face of statements by company leaders who defend their firm's questionable actions by claiming to be acting "in the best interests of the shareholders." If so, they have disparaged their own management ability and, perhaps, revealed a lack of concern for their own employees, customers and partners as well as the community in which they operate. Remarks like this also hint at a complete disregard for corporate and personal ethics.

Too harsh? Recall my proposed criterion for deciding who most deserves ethical behavior. Then apply it to the following groups.

Employees enable a company to exist. At its core, every business consists of a group of individuals working toward a common purpose within a defined infrastructure and with access to a source of capital. Who else qualifies more (with one exception) for totally ethical treatment? The exception would apply to underperforming employees who choose not, or are unable, to contribute to the company's success. It is not unethical to fire such individuals, although it is clearly desirable (and legally necessary) to treat them in an ethical manner.

Customers are near, or at par with, employees when it comes to importance. They provide purpose, direction and not least of all money to a business in the form of sales and profits. Some customers, it's true, can be demanding to the point of affecting a company's success and justifying the end of the relationship. This type of action varies widely in practice; an obstreperous customer or client is easier for Walmart to discard than for a small advertising agency, for example. On a surface level at least, however, unethical treatment of customers is perilous practice. An American Express study confirmed that U.S. shoppers resent companies that take customers for granted. In response, customers vote with their credit cards:[41]

- 75 percent feel that companies don't care about keeping their business
- 73 percent have spent more money with companies that treated them fairly
- 59 percent would switch brands or company to receive better service, despite higher prices and less convenience.

Vendors play a major role in every company's success, although the role may vary in size and intensity depending upon the nature of the business. Suppliers of commodities function differently from those supplying mechanical components to a manufacturer, for example. Nevertheless, ethical standards remain important, and a policy of building long-term relationships based on trust and honesty can generate serious dividends when a vendor/supplier is called upon for assistance in a crisis, such as an imposing delivery deadline. Ethical standards include the usual expectations, such as paying invoices within an agreed-upon schedule and avoiding demands to renegotiate a contract in the buyer's favor without any motive beyond greed. In recent years, vendors themselves have been called upon to set and confirm their own ethical standards, bringing them in line with their customers' principles. Apparel companies, for example, are demanding that suppliers maintain humane working conditions for those producing the garments, that animals be treated and transported humanely and that vendors minimize their impact on the environment. Is this going too far? Should American businesses be assigned the role of ensuring good working conditions and animal husbandry, for example, when the actions are two or three steps away from the product being sold?

The practical answers are No to the first question and Yes to the second, if our business principles are to be held in higher esteem than the pursuit of profits alone. Passing ethical standards down the supply chain generates ripples of responses, because higher business standards and practices will flow from the organization that leads with them. The concentric rings can have a positive effect on all the stakeholders they reach—customers, suppliers, partners and the broader community. Think about your own experiences and the results of the American Express study. Ethics cut both ways. Display a lack of them and expect to lose business and partners; demonstrate a strict code of ethics, and benefits will accrue in many ways on many levels.

Everywhere you look in business, the demand for ethics and the expectations of profits cross paths here and there. A generation or so ago, the act of maximizing profits was expected to win out over adhering to corporate values. Suppliers who sold on the basis of price and delivery were rarely questioned about their ability to do so, especially if the process involved semi-skilled labor and a foreign locale. That situation has changed in recent years, not as a result of a heightened sense of personal responsibility—everyone loves to buy an $8 T-shirt without being concerned about the welfare of the people who wove and sewed it—but in reaction to the availability and impact of graphic news reports.

In April 2013, an eight-story garment factory in Dhaka, Bangladesh, collapsed, crushing 1,130 people in the rubble. Hundreds more were severely crippled, many losing arms and legs that had to be amputated on the spot to save their lives. All had worked twelve-hour days and had been poorly paid. Workers in the section of the building that remained intact were ordered to ignore the screams of workers trapped under tons of stone and concrete and to remain at their job, producing inexpensive cotton clothing destined for North American retailers. The same workers had been frightened earlier by the constant shaking of the building and the deep visible cracks that appeared in the walls. Leaving their workstations, they had been warned, meant the loss of their jobs. To many, this meant no income for their families, and so they remained.[42]

When details of the disaster emerged, including the fact that the building had been illegally constructed using sub-standard materials, and that the wages earned by the workers varied between 24 and 33 cents *per hour*, the consumers who were the ultimate buyers of the clothing grew outraged. Manufacturing those $8 T-shirts, they realized, involved working conditions that affronted them. It took a horrific disaster to awaken them to the harsh reality behind their bargain purchases.

When media reports detailed the horror of the disaster, and that the decision to choose suppliers working in those conditions had been based on saving a few pennies in cost per garment, boycotts ensued. In response, one of the companies whose low-priced clothing brand was produced in the factory divorced itself from the offshore supplier and introduced a new set of ethical standards. These demanded that suppliers guarantee minimum standards in pay and working conditions, hoping to avoid a repeat of such an event. The clothing brand's sales began to recover and, within a year, were at or near the market share they had enjoyed earlier.

Among the most remarkable side effects of the company's decision to demand ethical standards of its suppliers was the financial impact of implementing those higher standards. In most cases, the increase in prices proved negligible, and the publicity of the parent company's much-heralded ethics was worth millions. While the impact of the Bangladesh tragedy sadly remains measured in missing limbs and broken families, the negative effect on the garment brand's image among its buyers has all but vanished, thanks to their attention to better business principles in the face of a crisis.

Communities, and their role in the operation and success of corporations, are less obvious when assessing ethical obligations, but no less important to consider. As with other stakeholders—especially employees and vendors—the benefits flow two ways. Large, successful companies generate employment and large quantities of tax revenue for communities. They may also, according to their largesse, contribute to vital facilities such as hospitals, colleges and recreational sites.

Benefits flow in the other direction as well. Immediate communities provide pools of employees and customers, plus essential infrastructure including roads, power, water, communications and other essentials. In ideal situations, these benefits are evenly balanced between the two entities, but the advantages provided by the community at large are easily taken for granted by the corporations that belong to it. Selling the role of communities short, and assuming that ethical principles need not apply to the towns and cities where major businesses hang their corporate hats, is simply wrong.

In light of the contributions of all five stakeholder groups, the passive involvement of shareholders becomes almost secondary in importance. Yet many business leaders continue to identify them as the group most deserving of attention and benefits.

Assessing good ethical standards, and how and where to apply them, may appear difficult. For most people, however, the simple solution is to assume a blanket policy—one that assumes everyone engaged in, or affected by, a business operation deserves to be treated in an equally ethically manner.

Earlier I quoted the 2,000-year-old wisdom of Marcus Aurelius, who advised people to stop debating goodness and simply be a good person. The inference is that we all know how to do it. Here's another thought from Aurelius to ponder. This one relates to maintaining standards and ethics when it comes to dealing with all stakeholders in a business: "That which is not good for the beehive cannot be good for the bees."

14

Integrity: The Difference between Leaders and Rulers

STRANGE THINGS ARE happening in hotels these days. They are changing their names. It began in Toronto in June 2017, when workers descended on a sixty-five-story luxury hotel and condominium and began yanking letters from the building's facade. The letters spelled Trump International Hotel and Tower. They were soon replaced with St. Regis Hotel, and all reference to Trump vanished.

Donald Trump had never owned the hotel. He licensed his name to it when the word *Trump* carried a certain cachet among a segment of people willing to spend several hundred dollars a night for a place to sleep. Almost from the building's opening date in 2012, few people were interested in staying there either overnight or as condo residents. For the 2016 Toronto International Film Festival, actors and producers attending the major industry event declined to stay there. "Anywhere but Trump" became a common directive from the Hollywood set who had no problem with the hotel's location, its staff, its amenities or anything else about the place—except its association with the man who a few weeks later became the forty-fifth president of the United States.*

* Within two years of opening, the Trump Tower was in receivership.

Word soon spread that Trump properties across America and elsewhere could expect to shed their identification with the man. In fact, a new line of hotels to be developed and managed by Ivanka Trump will be known as Scion, without her family name being revealed.* It's all a matter of association. Too many people want nothing to do with Trump—not just with him directly, but even with his name and all that is linked with it.

Think of that for a moment: The name of the president of the United States has such poor prestige associated with it that few people agree to patronize a business connected with him.

No one, including me, was overly surprised when Trump's reputation spilled over to tarnish anything bearing his name. It simply proved the premise that the people at the top of any organization dictate the image, and ultimately the success, of the business according to the public's perception of their values. In Trump's case, the impact was more powerful thanks to his high profile along with many of his outrageous antics and comments. It's clear that Donald Trump functions within his business organizations the same way he functions in the White House: he behaves as a ruler, not as a leader.

The difference between the two is significant. In many ways, it springs from the personal values of the person at the top, and the manner in which they treat those around them. As the following comparisons suggest, leaders demonstrate integrity and decency. Rulers exhibit neither.

Leaders listen and speak. Rulers command and control.

Leaders motivate. Rulers terrify.

Leaders become involved. Rulers remain remote.

Leaders correct. Rulers scold.

Leaders teach and learn. Rulers expect and ignore.

How many of these qualities of rulers can be associated with businesspeople of high integrity? I'm not suggesting that bosses or managers who remain remote from their employees, scold and terrify their staff and insist on controlling every activity also engage in illegal or immoral activities. That's a different metric where integrity

* Trump Hotels news release, September 28, 2016: "Trump Hotels Name New Lifestyle Brand Scion."

is concerned. Clearly, however, it is difficult to visualize that kind of behavior from someone who maintains high moral values, respects everyone with whom he or she works, and serves as a model of integrity for others.

Over and over again, Trump's statements and actions belie any assumption that he qualifies as a leader, by any definition of that term. He does, however, match the description of ruler, and I suspect he would be very pleased to wear that title. But here's the difficulty: As I write this, Donald Trump occupies the purported position of Leader of the Free World. It's from that position that he may, in the minds of some businesspeople, redefine the qualities necessary for leadership, replacing those listed above with disdain for anyone with an opposing view, a rejection of honest and open dealings, and the pursuit of profitability over decent behavior.

Let's come back to the factor of trust once more, another key measure of the ethical businessperson. Every leader's trustworthiness, according to one highly respected source, is based on three key pillars: their ability; their benevolence; and their integrity.[43] The link between integrity and trust cannot be overestimated in a leader's ability to inspire loyalty. Trust is associated with kindness and having good intentions rather than selfish motives. "Followers are willing to be vulnerable in a good way to leaders they trust," says the source, "and are more inclined to be satisfied with and committed to them."

I have worked with and closely observed many good leaders in business, and I'll be the first to attest to the impact they can make on an organization. I'm speaking not only of those leaders who aid their staff to achieve or exceed their goals, both private and corporate. The best leaders—those dedicated to integrity in all their actions and decency in all their relationships—go much further than that. Their influence is often subtle but powerful, especially on the wider objectives of the corporation.

For example, companies with effective and trusted leadership do not have to force or define their culture; it develops over time as a reflection of the values displayed by the leader. Everyone understands the vision and goals of the organization, knowing their input on applications and improvements will always be welcome. Promotions and rewards are made based on the most suitable abilities and experience. And the balance between everyone assisting coworkers to succeed, while performing at the best of their own ability in competition with others, is not seen as a contradiction but as a formula for collective success.

This may sound like some form of corporate utopia, a nirvana for HR executives and MBA scholars. But it's not. Examples of values-based CEOs who achieved outstanding success for their companies are not just easy to find—they're prominent in the business media. I'm speaking of people like Apple CEO Tim Cook, who agreed to forfeit half of his annual compensation in 2013 if Apple failed to outperform other S&P 500 companies. The promise cost him $4 million in income that year. And Whole Foods CEO John Mackey wrote a book titled *Conscious Capitalism: Liberating the Heroic Spirit of Business*, in which he proposed that American businesses must serve the interests of all major stakeholders, from customers, employees and investors to suppliers and communities. Along the way, he says, they should also make every effort to protect the environment. Mackey claims he has followed this dictum since cofounding his firm thirty-five years ago—a company, by the way, that he sold to Amazon for $13.7 billion in 2017.

Or consider this for proof: In 2015, the *Harvard Business Review* published a book titled *Return on Character: The Real Reason Leaders and Their Companies Win*, in which the author, Dr. Fred Kiel, collected data on eighty-four CEOs from their staff and salaried employees. He looked for confidential assessments of each CEO's value system—fairness, honesty, openness and all the other qualities I've been talking about. Then he cross-referenced the long-term performance of each company whose CEO rated highly for values and integrity against those whose ratings were lower.

The results were dramatic. Kiel discovered that companies with the highest values and integrity rating scored annual returns averaging 9.4 percent while those in the lower third had a yield of just 1.9 percent.[44] Let's call the difference between those two figures an impressive dividend earned as a result of enlightened CEOs acting not just out of integrity, but also recognizing the large number of contributors to their company's operations and success.

"You know the best thing about running things with a lot of integrity?" one highly admired CEO said. "It makes things easier. We don't question ourselves, and nobody asks, 'Should we, or shouldn't we?' There is no second-guessing and no hiding the truth, because it's always out there to see. Life becomes simple, and you live and work in peace."

And, I might add, if you and your reputation are associated with your business—say, a chain of hotels, for example—you might never have to deal with changing the company name.

15

Ethics: Define Them, Live Them

All leaders are models. But the best leaders don't rely exclusively on their personal conduct, as important as it may be in setting ethical standards. Codifying these standards helps ensure uniform behavior among everyone in the organization, especially when it comes to navigating through any ethical gray areas that might be encountered.

It's easy to become cynical about articulating a company's operating principles, particularly in a code of ethics. Many of us recall the rush for companies to draft, display and promote mission statements two or three decades ago. They were a good idea, but I always felt they were more inspired by fashion than fortitude. It seemed every business framed and displayed their mission statement in their reception area, where it became as noticeable as wallpaper. Those who took the time to scan the words encountered platitudes such as "focus on customer satisfaction," "promote high levels of community service" and "provide job satisfaction and fair compensation for employees and owners." Most were too wordy and too all-purpose, a once-size-fits-all collection of generalities.

The best mission statements are short and specific:

Comforting animals, confronting cruelty. —SPCA
To inspire conservation of the oceans.—MONTEREY BAY AQUARIUM
To create content that educates, informs and inspires. —PBS

Over time, mission statements lost whatever impact and credibility they may once have had simply because, among other things, employees rarely saw evidence that the company was adhering to them. Mission statements, after all, are like guidelines to healthy eating that tell us the foods we should consume every day and those we should avoid. We can, and probably will, break the "rules" now and then with a heaping plate of fries and a cholesterol-heavy milkshake or two. That's not a big deal where a diet is concerned. Nor is it if we take our eye off the company mission statement to pursue some promising off-the-wall opportunity, assuming the promise is real and the action is legal. But a code of ethics is a very different thing; a similar lapse in following ethical directives can prove disastrous.

Mission statements are created primarily to impress shareholders and customers, as well as to inspire employees, and a code of ethics can perform the same functions for the same groups. But when it comes to the corporation generally and its employees specifically, the purpose of a code of ethics is not to impress. It is to instruct. The guidelines within a code of ethics are not to be glanced at periodically; they are to be lived every day, in the same manner that we all live our lives according to social standards and legal guidelines. Codes of ethics are not intended to demand a higher standard but to translate principles into action, guiding everyday behavior and decision-making for all members of the organization. For this reason, a code of ethics should be succinct, direct and clear in its intent. Perhaps the oldest and best-known sample of the breed is the Hippocratic oath taken by physicians: First, do no harm.*

* Actually, the oft-quoted section of the oath reads: "I will apply dietetic measures for the benefit of the sick according to my ability and judgment; I will keep them from harm and injustice." It is instructive that this and other language from the oath have been distilled over the years to four simple words.

Ethics, by the way, are not laws. Obeying the law involves a form of conduct imposed by society and represents the minimal level of ethical measures required. You and your company can act entirely within prescribed laws yet clearly behave unethically. A pharmaceutical company that sets exceptionally high prices for an exclusive life-saving drug or medical treatment, purely in search of generating lofty undeserved profits, may operate legally, but its ethical standards would be open to question. Another example: It is unethical to lie, but doing so is illegal only while under oath. Had Donald Trump made many of his clearly untrue statements under oath, he would be subject to criminal prosecution and impeachment. The distinction is important. Drafting a code of ethics has little to do with establishing a system of laws and everything to do with a firm's commitment to filling the role of a good corporate citizen while in pursuit of profit. There is no contradiction to those two goals. Ever.

Four Reasons Why; Seven Steps to Take

Every corporation in America needs a code of ethics. Especially during an era in which the elected, legitimate leader of the country appears to have none... nor even to understand its role. Here are four important reasons that I have gleaned from my own experience and from nearly a half century of working among companies that either benefited from the existence of a code or suffered from the absence of one.

REASON #1: BUILDING A REPUTATION FOR ETHICAL BEHAVIOR HELPS BUILD CUSTOMER LOYALTY

Customers have become fickle thanks to the impact of social media and investigative journalism. Their loyalty to one brand, supplier or retail source can vanish with the first appearance of a policy or incident that even suggests a lack of ethics or fairness.

It's not just the incident itself that can cause problems; it's also the breadth and tone of coverage. Back to that unfortunate United

Airlines passenger being dragged down the aisle with his mouth bleeding, his glasses askew and other passengers wearing horrified expressions.

United acted legally but unethically. Some observers point to the small print on every airline ticket that grants the carrier a right to ban and remove any passenger. Very nice, and I'm sure the lawyers were pleased. But that's legality, not ethics. No conceivable excuse exists to physically injure an otherwise benign passenger, strapped in a paid-for seat, solely to satisfy the airline's need to seat others—in this case, crew members traveling to another United destination.

Ethical behavior must be practiced not only to build customer loyalty, but also to prevent it from eroding due to unforeseen and unavoidable situations. Sometimes ethical heroics are invisible and unacknowledged. They occur because they are the right thing to do, and following any other course of action risks damaging your reputation for playing fair.

The biggest barrier to maintaining ethical standards, or going beyond them when appropriate, is undue concern over the bottom line. In case it need be said: *Profitability is the prime goal for any business to set and achieve*. But excessive focus on maximizing profitability in the short term is almost always disastrous. Going in the other direction, however, can build dividends far beyond the original cost.

Here's an example: A rental car company—not a giant like Hertz, Enterprise or Budget—received a call from a customer who had driven one of its vehicles to Tennessee in July. The customer reported that she had been involved in a minor accident. Thankfully unhurt, she called to say that, as a result of the incident, her driver's door wouldn't close properly. It was a sweltering and rainy day; the air conditioning couldn't reduce the temperature enough and rain poured into the car as she drove. The car rental company had no office in Tennessee or an adjacent state.

The response was immediate: Two employees of the company drove a similar vehicle nonstop over eight hundred miles to the woman's location in Knoxville, handed over the keys and paperwork, and brought the original car back to the franchise office. They did this without checking with head office or seeking special permission. It was simply a matter of acting in an ethical manner on behalf of a customer.[45]

I don't know how much the trip cost the car rental company in out-of-pocket expenses. I will almost guarantee that the customer won't seriously consider renting a car from anyone else in the future. Nor, I suspect, will the friends and business associates who hear about the incident from her.

By the way, some people may hear of this story and say, "That's not ethical behavior—it's just good business sense!"

To which I reply: "And your point is?"

REASON #2: ETHICAL BUSINESSES ATTRACT AND KEEP GOOD EMPLOYEES

Behaving ethically isn't a selective process; you can't behave like angels in the presence of your customers and act like devils when dealing with employees. Some staff members may put up with it, but not for long. Nor can you expect an abysmally treated employee to act in a totally gracious and understanding manner to customers.

Companies that foster ethical behavior generate a parallel response from their staff. Imagine working in a company where top-level managers make public speeches that are patently untrue; where their manipulation of tax laws in favor of corporate profits is an open secret; and where promises to employees are either broken or simply ignored. Compare this with working in an environment where everyone is treated fairly, openly and equally, creating ripple-effect dividends for stakeholders within and beyond the organization. You would logically expect that employees at lower levels in these two situations would behave very differently, given the contrasting actions of their leaders. You don't even have to be working at a firm to have its ethical behavior influence your own. Psychologically, it's far more difficult to lie or exaggerate your qualifications during a job interview with a firm known for its ethical standards than for an organization whose values are loose and whose reputation is sketchy.

REASON #3: GOOD ETHICS CREATE A POSITIVE WORKING ENVIRONMENT

It's a funny thing about people working among associates they trust: everyone works harder and more efficiently. Never underestimate the impact of trust among those who work, play or live together.

It's easy to trust a colleague when you know that both of you are aware of and following rules that stem from common values. In an environment where the members trust those around them, confidential information remains secure, teamwork is easily achieved, and on-the-job behavior is in tune with corporate goals. Assuming salary and wage levels are competitive within the industry, it's difficult for an employee to risk losing a job like that. And here's another dividend: companies have never been more aware of the cost of recruiting and training employees to replace those who might resign because they don't enjoy their work or feel their own values are at odds with those being demonstrated by management. If fostering a culture of shared corporate values and ethics helps you hold onto experienced and dedicated employees who enjoy their work, that's more than effective management. It's a means of achieving maximum efficiency and profits.

REASON #4: IT KEEPS YOU OUT OF COURT

I am no fan of regulations. Who is? But as long as they are on the books for a good reason, breaking the rules to make an extra buck or two is foolish.

I could fill this book with all the ways of ignoring regulations while expecting your competitors to obey them. They include scoffing at environmental concerns, disregarding employee safety standards, breaking labor laws, using unhealthy product components, engaging in illegal securities trading and others. If you consider some regulations unfair or discriminatory, find ways to have them repealed or modified through industry associations and legislative means. Otherwise, comply with them, or risk denting your bottom line with fines and other sanctions plus massive legal costs. And it doesn't stop there. Most of us prefer not to be associated with companies and brand names clouded with negative publicity. Need proof? Check the sales of vw cars since the scandal covered in Chapter 5, or the drop-off in United Airline's traffic and earnings as the result of their unfair treatment of a passenger discussed in Chapter 13.

Seven Steps to a Meaningful Code

Writing a code of ethics isn't as challenging as writing a novel, or even a business book promoting ethical behavior. It does, however, demand attention to detail on the expectations of management, staff and employees.

Here are my guidelines for preparing a code of ethics for your firm. I propose seven; you may wish to add some, depending on your company's circumstances. I wouldn't subtract any, however, without giving deep thought to the implications.

STEP 1: MAKE IT INDUSTRY-SPECIFIC, IF NECESSARY

"Honesty is the best policy" is a given when it comes to ethics. Some aspects of every business, however, deserve specific reference. Food processing companies deal with different ethical issues than those associated with technological service organizations or railroads, for example. It's unlikely that computer programmers will need to be as focused on meeting standards for hygiene as a producer of pasta sauce, nor will they be concerned about addressing the same concern for preventing industrial accidents as a railroad.

What about size? Are some companies simply too small to go on record about their ethical standards? Quick answer: No. Longer, more detailed answer: Never.

STEP 2: BE CONCISE

Less is more. Being specific to your firm's industry or situation does not equate to being verbose. Create a comprehensive code that is succinct enough to fit on one sheet of standard-sized paper. Yes, it can be done. It takes time and skill to say more with fewer words. But it can be done.

STEP 3: SEEK INPUT

It makes no sense to invest time and effort writing a code of ethics if the principles you list fail to elicit support from employees. You need buy-in across the board, which means seeking input from every level in the company before drafting the code. This includes discovering and dealing with potential ethical challenges that may be encountered by employees. Dictating strict rules from the top down without asking for input is like handing out commandments carved in stone. The original Ten Commandments at least benefited from deep respect for their source. Pursuing employee input prior to approval will avoid resentment and improve the chance of a rule receiving broad support.

An ideal way to get started: announce that you are drafting the code, list the company's core values and ask for confidential comments on situations that have made staff members uneasy about the ethical factors involved. You'll not only build broader participation, you may also discover startling ethical incidents that your employees face from time to time.

STEP 4: DON'T NITPICK

Offering kickbacks or seeking bribes are actions that should never be tolerated. Accepting a plate of holiday cookies from a supplier is hardly the same issue. Keep things in perspective; sweating the small stuff is sure to generate hostility and resentment. It's better to focus on your organization's fundamental values and on capturing the spirit of the feedback you receive when drafting the code.

STEP 5: DON'T DUCK THE DIFFICULT ISSUES

Not all ethical issues within a business are cut-and-dried. What do you do, for example, about romantic relationships among employees? State and federal labor and employment laws will address some ethical dilemmas. It's worth stating within your firm's code that you will adhere to them, especially when addressing discrimination, harassment and sexual misconduct. Where none of these legal guidelines is present, consider a policy that speaks, for example, to the potential problem of two staff members engaged in a long-term relationship.

Is it tolerated? Will one member be dismissed? Or will everything be judged on a case-by-case basis? This will likely avert resentment and bitterness when both parties know what is involved from the beginning... and if the policy is applied fairly and equally.

And let's be honest: some situations cannot be dealt with through a code alone. Is nepotism an unethical practice? Of course, but only if the hired or promoted individual is chosen solely on his or her family association. That's an indefinable quality for a written code, but the existence of a code itself makes the situation palatable. Promoting someone from within a family is much more acceptable to other employees when they consider management to be scrupulous about their actions in other areas.

STEP 6: SEEK HELP CAREFULLY

Should you seek legal assistance in drafting a code of ethics? Yes and no. Yes, because lawyers can act as a sounding board, a fresh eye to spot potential problem areas—conflicts with legislated guidelines, for example—that you may not be aware of. This may be especially valuable when integrating employee submissions, where little thought has been given to legal ramifications. No, because lawyers see their role as interpreters of actions, focusing on what can be defended in court. So it's wise to limit their involvement to ensuring compliance with appropriate state and federal laws. Remember: unethical actions are not necessarily illegal.

STEP 7: PUT SOMEONE IN CHARGE

Ethical behavior may be everyone's concern, but applying and updating the code should be an individual's assignment. Finance and investment companies are required to retain compliance officers whose goal is to ensure that fixed guidelines are followed in each transaction. You don't have to go that far, but it's wise to designate someone whose responsibilities include reviewing and updating the code of ethics as required.

This step prevents the code from being just another memo or directive. It becomes alive and dynamic, something for employees to be aware of and respect. Identifying a trusted individual who is accountable for monitoring the code and taking whatever initial steps are needed if a compliance problem arises adds to the document's power.

BUSINESS CONSULTANTS HAVE been advising for years that owners and executives should draft a short, company-specific code of ethics free of jargon and widely supported throughout the organization. Given the changing legal and social climate these days, especially with regards to dealing with sexism and racism, it seems like a prudent move. It also represents a critical step in developing and nurturing a values-based culture that adds immeasurably to a company's chance for success. With such a move comes the promise of dividends earned from principled standards and decent actions.

16

Diversity: The Secret Ingredient of Successful Companies

DONALD TRUMP'S ACTIONS and comments about women make it clear that he does not respect them. He appears to be equally dismissive of Latinos, his early activities as a New York landlord hint at distrust and dislike of African-Americans, and his support for white supremacists has been nothing less than offensive.

American business cannot claim acceptable ethical standards as long as it tolerates disrespect for, and discrimination against, any individuals or groups in the workplace. In fact, in my opinion, American business will match its history of leading the world in progress and achievement not by just *tolerating* diversity but only by *embracing and promoting* it.

I suspect this idea will create pushback from some quarters where diversity of race, gender, skin color, age, sexual preference, national origin and religion are considered root causes for internal conflict. The issues of race and intolerance for minorities remain stubbornly entrenched within some quarters of the business community. Moreover, the impact of intolerance and discrimination is growing. In just one example, research indicates that African-American males not only experience one of the highest levels of unemployment in America but that their plight grows more disastrous with the passage of time.[46] During the Trump era, discrimination against Latinos and Muslims rose dramatically as a direct result of his haranguing them. This is beyond intolerable; it is inherently destructive to both American business and American society generally.

Similarly, the glass ceiling is still very much an issue for women in this country, when they are denied access to top-level executive or board positions. Let me put it in a more direct and personal perspective: should my wife, Cayce—or any woman with similar capabilities—encounter rejection pursuing a senior management position at a large corporation, a distinct possibility exists that the decision would be based at least partly on her gender. I am not proposing some system of gender-based affirmative action; only that gender (and race, religion and other factors as well) must be dismissed when assessing ability in the workplace.

Accepting people for who and what they are, and hiring and promoting them based on ability and merit, is a more direct and harmonious path to business success than perpetuating barriers and conflict in the workplace. I would think that this sort of wisdom is commonplace in 2017. It should be. Unfortunately, the actions and attitudes modeled by Donald Trump distort this principle in the minds of too many Americans. Including, sad to say, executives at various levels in various corporations.

It needn't be that way. I recall reading an interview with a professional football coach several years ago. Some observers were questioning the balance of African-American players versus white players. Was one group being favored against others, suggesting that athletic ability came second to skin color? When the question was put to the highly respected and tough-minded football coach, his response was instant and convincing: "Ask me how many halfbacks I have, and I can tell you right away," he replied. "Ask me how many African-Americans I have, and I'll have to go into the locker room and count them."

If that doesn't put things into perspective, here are two quotes from very different sources: "Diversity is the art of thinking differently together" and "It takes many different flowers to make a beautiful bouquet." The first quote is from Malcolm Forbes. You needn't agree with everything he says, but you have to grant that he speaks from a pro-business perspective. The other quote is a Muslim proverb, making it doubly appropriate in this context.

The Risk of Employees "Working It Out" for Themselves

Surely the least important factor in evaluating work performance is cultural identity, or anything else that makes an individual "different." Mutual respect in the workplace must be based on respect for abilities and skills, not on suspicion or outright prejudice. Owners and managers who tolerate any measure of prejudice against a productive employee are damaging the basis of success and profitability. Disrespect of others in the workplace, whether it be expressed openly or covertly, seriously damages cooperation and synergy.

It's a given—everyone works more efficiently in an environment of mutual respect and tolerance. Anyone in a position of authority who responds to conflicts based on disrespect for the values and origins of others by advising them to "work it out among yourselves" is not only abdicating responsibility. He or she is fostering a continuance of destructive behavior. "Work it out" invariably leads either to the minority group or individual giving in to the majority's opinion and directives, or concealing the problem beneath a thin surface of fake tolerance that eventually shreds. Either way, tension remains and productivity suffers.

This can lead to the nonsensical premise among some that homogeneity is a key to success in business. Surely, they assume, groups in and out of business function more effectively and with less conflict when they all share similar values and goals. Isn't that what America once was, a melting pot in which everyone shared the same language, heritage and religion? Oh yes—and gender as well?

I don't believe America was ever quite like that, except in Norman Rockwell paintings and feel-good Hollywood movies. But it doesn't matter. Like it or not, America (and much of the rest of the Western world) is composed of people from a potpourri of backgrounds. Going backward is not an option. And dealing with the diversity engrained in most societies and organizations today is not just a necessity—it's an opportunity.

Leaders are key to encouraging and promoting diversity in the organization. It is their role and responsibility to ensure that the company's ethical values become the moral compass for decent behavior throughout the workplace. Permitting the values of any one group within the company to hold sway will lead to discord, resentment and lack of productivity. One more time: The primary function of leaders—business, political, military—is to inspire those around them. Failure to perform this function, especially when it comes to inspiring others to tolerate differences in culture and race, is self-defeating.

When it comes to making a point, I have always believed that the simpler the language the better. So here's my summation on the subject: Racism and intolerance are not only wrong—they're stupid.

Based on my own experience in business and researching the subject from multiple sources, I've created a list of dividends to be earned from promoting diversity in the workplace. They include:

- *Success attracting and retaining talent*, adding both a competitive edge and an advantage for companies wanting to expand their operations in global markets.
- *Productivity increases,* as a result of different talents applying different sets of skills to specific challenges.
- *Greater creativity and problem-solving abilities* from a diverse range of experiences and cultural viewpoints.
- *Prospects of increasing market share* and building a diverse, satisfied customer base by relating to people from different backgrounds, both within the company and in its various market regions.
- *Opportunities to build synergy and communication skills* that profit the entire team.
- *Elimination of potential litigation expenses* generated by discrimination-based lawsuits, simply by "doing the right thing."

People from diverse backgrounds bring important, different and competitively relevant knowledge and perspectives to their work. Much of this is down-to-earth practical understanding about how to actually *do work*—how to implement processes, design products, reach goals, frame tasks, create effective teams, communicate ideas and, in some cases, provide leadership. It's true that some unique points of view and talents may challenge basic assumptions about the organization's goals, policies, practices and processes. It's also true that not every new proposal proves wholly practical and ultimately rewarding. But guess what? There are no guarantees of success in business. There are, however, guarantees for failure, and they involve steadfast attitudes that say "We've always done things this way" and "We don't need to look at new ideas." These kinds of observations are usually followed, somewhere down the line, with comments like "Now why didn't we think of that?"

The Dividends of Diversity

All this talk of nurturing an inclusive work environment may remind hard-nosed businesspeople of sitting around a campfire, holding hands and singing "Kumbaya"—in other words, something intended to make us feel good but that has little to do with polishing the bottom line. Well, it's not true. Practical confirmation of the benefits of encouraging tolerance and diversity in the workplace exists. The data is valued and paraded with pride by companies whose policies reflect the practice.

A company appropriately called DiversityInc. measures the actions of participating firms that promote diversity among their staff and employees. In a recent study, the research firm identified the top fifty American companies rated according to their policies related to fostering diversity among their employees at every management level. The list of firms ranged from health care giant Kaiser Permanente (rated tops for its policies) and communications powerhouse AT&T, to familiar hospitality names (Marriott International, Hilton, Wyndham), major pharmaceutical manufacturers (Johnson

& Johnson, Eli Lilly), financial institutions (Prudential, TD Bank, MassMutual, Mastercard) and several other categories.[47]

Of the companies rated in the Top 50 category, forty-two were publicly traded. Drilling into their financial performance revealed that companies with exceptionally high levels of diversity scored a 24.8 percent higher return than the S&P 500 when measured over ten years with dividends reinvested. An earlier study looked at the 353 companies among the Fortune 500 who had the highest proportion of women on their executive-leadership teams. Over four out of five years during the period studied, return on equity for these firms was 35 percent higher, and total return to shareholders was 34 percent higher, compared with companies that had the lowest representation of female leaders.[48] And Nextel Communications Inc. achieved a return on investment of 163 percent on their diversity training investment, thanks to improved retention and more efficient employee performance.[49] When was the last time your company scored a return of 163 percent on an investment, of any kind?

When American businesses view diversity holistically and value its ability to deliver fresh and meaningful methods of reaching goals, they will reap all the dividends it offers. Not just for them. But for America itself.

17

Values and the Future of American Business

I'M NO FUTURIST, and I understand the folly of attempting to predict how things will change over the next five, ten and twenty years. Some outcomes, however, appear obvious. If you don't believe the next generation will be riding around in driverless cars, you probably wouldn't have believed that the Wright Brothers put a contraption in the air in Kitty Hawk, North Carolina.

On the business front, I suggest that the impact of changes on the horizon will be more powerful in their effect than anything in the past 150 years. Wider globalization, extended automation of business-related functions and the effects of fluid international trade policies will influence business operations at a dizzying rate. Along with these, corporations will be capable of exercising power and influence to a frightening degree. The impact on business ethics from all of these developments is difficult to predict, but given the current "role model" in the White House, I fear it will be a slippery slope downward. Trump's America represents the unfettered pursuit of profits (at the expense of principles and ethical values) and ever-increasing power for the corporate sector (at the expense of government regulations and oversight).

In an age of disruptive change, we will need the touchstone of values and ethics more than ever as a positive influence to guide us through a world in constant flux. Shifting social patterns and values will create a need to reinforce fundamental principles that allow us to function harmoniously and effectively as a society. And in the world of business, values-based leadership can offer the constant we need at a time when technology is changing at ever-increasing speed, upending the fortunes of companies on a dime. If you think I'm exaggerating, come back with me to 1998 and we'll check out the status of two well-known American companies back then.

In 1998, almost everyone who took pictures—from folks capturing candid snapshots and vacation photos to Hollywood producers and Paris fashion photographers—used film as the sole medium. Not just any brand; they chose Kodak almost exclusively. Much film technology was over one hundred years old, involving plastic-based film and chemically treated paper. Kodak owned 85 percent of the film market and employed 170,000 people worldwide, dominating its industry beyond the measure of almost every other brand in history. Taking pictures meant using film, and buying film meant choosing Kodak. Yet within three years, the film industry virtually vanished and Kodak began its steep slide into bankruptcy.*

Now think of another company that was also operating in 1998. Its name was Apple. Things were very different in the computer industry back then. The largest PC names were Dell, Hewlett-Packard, IBM and Compaq. All were highly profitable and well-regarded. Apple, in contrast, had been drifting toward irrelevance for years. CEOs had been changing almost annually and the company lacked a viable product. Steve Jobs returned to the company he had cofounded twenty years earlier and began exerting his muscle. Many stories exist to explain Jobs's impact. Most note that Jobs didn't just resurrect Apple; he spawned an entire industry that carried consumer computing and electronics into uncharted territory with the iMac, iPhone, iPod and

* Ironically, Kodak originally invented digital photography in 1975. The company's failure to make the most of it over the next twenty-five years marks one of the great examples of a lost opportunity.

other products. By 2017, Apple was generating profits—not gross sales, *net profits*—at the rate of $3.6 million per hour, 24 hours per day, 365 days a year. Their cash reserve—not capitalization but cash on hand in various locations around the world—was estimated at almost $250 billion.[50]

Twenty years ago, no one could have imagined that an industry Goliath like Kodak could vanish in less than a generation. And no one would believe that a small California company well past its original best-before date would amass enough cash to pay every man, woman, child and cocker spaniel in the world more than US$30 and still have enough cash in the bank to buy them all a coffee as well.

Apple is admittedly a unique story of accelerated growth and success. It may not be unique for long, however. We are living in an era of accelerated change unmatched in history. Apple's success admittedly emerged from the creative mind and personality of one individual, but Steve Jobs's influence on young product developers and entrepreneurs has not been lost on them. Few may match or exceed him in his impact on business, but crowds of them will follow his example, launching innovations far wider in scope and numbers.

Consider these verifiable aspects of reality in 2017:

- The largest taxi company in the world (Uber), by revenue, owns no vehicles.
- The largest hotel company in the world (Airbnb), by revenue, owns no properties.
- It is widely agreed that the profession most likely to shrink and virtually vanish within two generations is the practice of law. Computer software is already over 90 percent accurate in determining legal status; human lawyers score barely 70 percent accuracy. Moreover, computers perform the drudge work of law not just more accurately but far more speedily. Think of the impact this will have on legal fees alone.
- After lawyers, the medical profession will find itself either shrinking in size or drastically altered in function. Computers are currently four

times more successful in diagnosing cancer than humans. They are also growing more adept at completing surgical procedures with lower failure rates (read: fatality rates) than humans.

- Among other effects of all-electric self-driving cars will be a reduction of accidents and injuries by 90 percent or more. Computer programs do not drive drunk or tired, and redundancy will virtually eliminate failures, either mechanical or programmable.
- Fewer cars will be built, sold and owned, thanks to lower maintenance needs (see previous bullet) and the opportunity to call for a car at will and leave it at your destination. What will happen to parking lots, garages and auto insurance companies?[51]

In the midst of so much change, in what I suspect will be a surprisingly concentrated amount of time, the role of leadership may well undergo drastic changes. Many traditional aspects of a leader's role in business—including market assessment, visionary capabilities and performance assessment—will be assumed by technology. And much of the success of a business organization will likely be judged by its wider role, both within the community where it functions and the society to which it appeals.

So what are the steadying influences? What business characteristics are most likely to remain valued, required and perhaps more necessary than ever? Things like Trust. Ethics. Honesty. Openness. Fairness.

The Demand for Ethics and Values

I have no doubt that in the time I have spent writing this book, a dozen or so innovators were taking their first major steps in launching a product or service capable of eclipsing Apple. And while you're reading this, they may be on their way toward achieving success on a similar scale. On that assumption, it's fair to ask: Who will deal with whom in developing, designing, marketing, promoting and profiting from these new ventures? Taking it a step further: Who will trust whom? Where waters are untested and potential financial returns are magnified, questions of values, ethics and trust become critical.

How comfortable would you be about entering into a first-time partnership with a Russia-based petroleum company today? Or a Sudanese gold mining company? Imagine making a business deal with partners in countries similar to them, but instead of dealing in oil and gold, the product promises to develop into an entirely new industry valued in tens of billions of dollars.

Fortunately, American business does not suffer from the same prevalent corruption commonly found in countries such as Russia or Sudan. At least not yet. But future seismic shifts in business will not only test the principles and values of American corporations; they will also lead to a new breed of partnerships, in which trust and ethics will matter even more than today. If American businesses reflect moral values on a level comparable with those that Donald Trump exhibits, how much will it limit this country's opportunities?

Technology, and the insistence of people who honor truth more than secrets, may make the difference. Social media, for all of its dangers and drawbacks, can serve as a balance against spin masters and promoters of "alternative facts" where needed. WikiLeaks, for example, is just the beginning of guerrilla strategies when it comes to assessing sovereign and corporate behavior. If your firm functions in the public arena, prepare yourself and your company to forget about controlling your personal and corporate reputations from the top down.

Remember the appalling loss of life due to the collapse of the building that housed sweat-shop operations in Bangladesh? The tragedy linked corruption, poverty, greed, class conflict and human rights violations into one heart-rending package. The brand names associated with the operation, including JCPenney, Walmart, Benetton and others, may have been some distance removed according to geography and liability, but they shared responsibility in the eyes of the public and large numbers of their customers. The long-term effects were significant. Many clothing firms employing cheap labor in Bangladesh, India, Malaysia and other corners of the developing world implemented a policy of demanding specific working conditions to be followed by contractors manufacturing their goods.

In a world dedicated to globalization, despite the hiccups of Brexit, Trump and others, we can expect to see greater awareness of, and demand for, ethical considerations by companies, regardless of their location and culture. Notwithstanding the new low bar that has been set for society and business by Donald Trump's presidency, I hope and believe that the tide is turning and that America's need and desire for fundamental human decency will win the day. Consider some trends we are already witnessing:

WIDER PARTICIPATION OF WOMEN IN ALL ASPECTS OF WESTERN LIFE

Women may rightly point out the existence of glass ceilings and their continued absence in corporate boardrooms (not to mention Donald Trump's cabinet). The lack of meaningful leadership opportunities for women is well established. But so is a growing intolerance for sexist practices and attitudes among male leaders. Although we cannot expect Donald Trump to serve as any kind of role model for this enlightened behavior, we can expect the generation of males born after 2000 to strike a more understanding attitude toward fairness and women's rights than their fathers and grandfathers.

GREATER ACCOUNTABILITY AND TRANSPARENCY FOR CORPORATE POLICIES

Progress on this front is slow as well, but I believe it is also inevitable. While we are unlikely to witness future legislation as wide-ranging and significant as the *Sarbanes-Oxley Act*, it may not be necessary. The impact of social media continues to grow and flourish, and a few well-placed, well-timed and well-expressed remarks on Facebook, Twitter and other social media platforms carry as much authority as almost any legislation Congress may enact. America's corporations will increasingly be held accountable in the court of public opinion.

DEMAND FOR HONESTY IN MARKETING AND PROMOTION

Social media is even more effective at demanding honesty in consumer transactions than in issues of corporate compliance. After all, few consumers venture into board meetings, but everyone visits malls and websites. Consumers have always voted with their wallets, but in the age of social media the influence of customers, and their values, on every company's bottom line will be on an entirely new level of magnitude.

UNFORESEEN NEW WAYS TO WORK AND DO BUSINESS GENERALLY

The concept of being compensated for work with wages and salaries appears to be doomed. An upsurge of "gigs"—limited-time employment arranged via contracts—may represent the future. Any looser work arrangement for businesses will continue to depend on the existence and application of measures involving trust and honesty. With no anticipated protection and representation from trade unions, as one likely event, how will individuals choose the firms to contract with, and to what extent will companies fulfill their obligations?

THE RIPPLE EFFECTS of these trends, coupled with some of the more dramatic technological advances and impacts mentioned earlier, will be substantial. And all may well occur and grow amid a renewed shift toward globalization. As the idea regenerates and gains momentum, one of the key expectations of all involved will be general consistency among major players. Countries and corporations alike will be forced to choose between meeting standards of quality in both their products and operating practices, or watch large market forces pass them by.

Among the qualities demanded of an international corporation will be a reputation for honesty, fairness, good ethics and, to a large degree, even the location of the company's home operations. In recent years, we have seen countries such as China, Myanmar, Russia and others suffer economic consequences based on their reputation for poor or nonexistent ethical standards. Where will America stand through all the changes of the coming years?

18

Why Trust Matters

As every parent knows, sometimes the simplest questions are the most difficult to answer. Children ask, "Why is the sky blue?" and "Where did I come from?" To my surprise, some businesspeople actually ask, "Why does trust matter?" Those who pose this question, I assume, are more philosophical than sincere. The answer appears obvious, especially to anyone who has dealt with a business partner who couldn't be trusted. But perhaps we need to ask the question anyway, if only to have the answers carry the weight they deserve. And sometimes the answer isn't just philosophical—it is practical and measured.

It also depends on the environment. Donald Trump, in my estimation, has so warped the fabric of American society (both generally and in a business context) that the question of trust needs to be addressed in a world influenced by the trickeries of Trump. For many years, a portion of Americans have drummed the message, over and over, that America needed a businessperson in the White House. Well, we got one. Unfortunately, his bona fides as a businessman were twisted by the appalling absence of basic ethics and values that I have itemized throughout this book. In the age of Trump, the businessman-cum-president, we need more than ever to consider the imperative of creating and maintaining trust in business generally.

Why does trust matter?

1. Because the amount of trust placed by the public in business represents the degree of vulnerability that the public is willing to assume in their transactions. The greater the level of trust that Americans grant business, the more they will rely on businesses to help them achieve their goals.
2. Because trusted companies are more profitable, better managed, highly rated and less likely to face litigation based on their business practices.
3. Because a sufficiently low degree of public trust in business leads to the introduction of often punitive regulations. As an example, the annual cost to American businesses of regulatory compliance post–*Sarbanes-Oxley* is an estimated $1.1 trillion, or almost 8 percent of GDP. The same study revealed that implementing one clause (Section 404) alone costs American businesses $35 billion annually.[52] Let's remember that the *Sarbanes-Oxley Act* was introduced in response to government, investor and public outrage at unethical actions taken by executives of Enron, WorldCom, Tyco, HealthSouth and other disgraced corporations.

Think about that last point: Every publicly traded company in America effectively pays an annual fine on behalf of executives who believed that ethical standards blocked their way to accruing enormous personal gain. After all, they thought, who needs trust, integrity, reputation and self-respect when you can add another million or $10 million or $100 million to your income or the company's bottom line?

Here's the shocker: top executives, and the companies they lead, can increase their earnings and profits not by discarding or lowering their ethical standards but by elevating and adhering to them. If this sounds like an oversimplified Sunday school lesson ("Be good and ye shall be blessed"), it's not. It is reality, confirmed and demonstrated by individuals and corporations who cash a Trust Dividend year after year.

Paying the Low-Trust Tax, Collecting the High-Trust Dividend

A 2002 study by Watson Wyatt revealed that widely trusted publicly traded companies generated a blended (stock price plus dividends) return to shareholders 286 percent higher than organizations with low levels of trust.[53] That's a pretty significant way to generate almost three times the return to shareholders.

Don't care for statistics? Use logic instead.

When it comes to doing business at almost any level, trust affects speed and cost. Your own business experience will confirm this fact. When trust is low between two partners in a transaction, speed drops and costs rise. For example, low trust demands deeper due diligence and greater involvement by legal counsel, auditors and others before deals are finalized. The source of extra costs to at least one party should be obvious. Conversely, when trust between the two sides is high, speed rises and costs fall. That's a Trust Dividend.

Warren Buffett, the paragon of principles and the dean of value investing, can attest to the existence of a Trust Dividend. When Berkshire Hathaway acquired McLane Company from Walmart in 2003, the basic deal was reached in a meeting that lasted barely two hours and was sealed with a handshake. Buffett described the mechanics behind the deal in his firm's annual report the following year. "We did no due diligence," he wrote, explaining how the deal came together so quickly. "We knew everything would be exactly as Walmart said it would be—and it was." This, by the way, was no nickel-and-dime venture. Buffett and his company handed over $23 billion for McLane. Deals that large normally take several months and a regiment of lawyers and accountants to pave the way. In this case, all the necessary paperwork was drafted, signed and certified in less than a month.[54]

Now imagine structuring such a deal with Donald Trump, aware of his reputation for making commitments he fails to keep, for using various dubious strategies to avoid paying debts, and for generally insisting that he emerge a total winner in the deal by out-maneuvering you with fancy footwork and exaggerated figures and estimates. Not to mention his penchant for launching lawsuits at the hint of a slight.

Trust Dividends can be earned and paid in several ways:

- **Fast sustained growth:** Customers may buy more products and services, refer their satisfaction to friends and clients, and remain more loyal to the company and brand.
- **Greater collaboration:** Companies with low levels of acknowledged trust may have difficulty finding partners to cooperate with them; those with high levels of trust will discover partners eager to collaborate, which is a far more productive arrangement.
- **Superior innovation:** Creativity thrives in an atmosphere of trust and atrophies in one of misgivings. All innovation begins with a creative act.
- **Increased value:** The cumulative impact of high levels of trust in all quarters is higher perceived and actual value for publicly traded companies. (See the Watson Wyatt reference above.)
- **Powerful partnering:** Business relationships at all levels gain strength when all sides hold others in equal trust; misgivings are slow to arise, and missteps are quickly understood and eliminated as threats.
- **Heightened loyalty:** Companies that embody high levels of trust inspire loyalty among individuals at every level and in every corner of their business operations, including stakeholders, employees, customers, suppliers, distributors and investors.

Everyone loves dividends. No one enjoys paying tax. Manage yourself and your company with ethics and high values, and you stand to earn a Trust Dividend. Alternatively, consider Donald Trump as the archetype of a businessperson and employ his antics, and expect to pay a Low-Trust Tax.

I SPOKE TO several people before writing this book, and when I discussed its premise, many replied, "So you're doing a book on politics?" I assured them that I wasn't. I have never been much of a political animal. I have always supported the importance of business in American life and the way business is conducted at every level, no matter the size of the organization. My concern about the state of business ethics in Donald Trump's America has nothing to do with partisan politics. But anyone who demands that the rest of society, including those duly elected in opposition, must agree and endorse his or her actions and objectives has no concept of what democracy means and how it should be practiced.

Trump has his supporters, I agree. They show up at his re-election rallies, which he launched within a few weeks of his inauguration. These people undoubtedly have their reasons for declaring their allegiance to Trump despite so many examples of his inability to deal with truth and reality, his admitted lack of understanding of government procedures, and his generally uncouth attitudes and lack of scruples. They may explain their support for him in various ways—they like his anti-establishment attitude, or they believe that only he listens to their grievances. Another explanation may be cognitive dissonance: when your deeply held principles conflict with your perception of reality, you change reality and not your beliefs.

We should all be concerned about Trump's ever-moving target when it comes to facts and truth, and about his virtually nonexistent ethics and their potential impact on American business. Now and in the turbulent years ahead, America's businesses need a strong moral compass. Donald Trump's power and influence affect all of us and our collective perception of what is right and acceptable. Even those who did not vote for Trump and generally oppose his views may still view his presence and position as passive approval to act in a similar manner—devoid of values, dedicated to self-promotion, dismissive and insulting toward other points of view, and focused exclusively on building personal net worth and ego.

Others have pointed out Trump's disregard for anything approaching the values that defined America for more than two hundred years. But rebuke is no longer enough. We have reached the point where each sector of American society must act to repudiate Trump's perverted sense of values. Some may choose to confine their actions to the political sphere, using censure, impeachment or election defeat to remove Trump from office. My choice has been to alert America to the ripple effect his low ethical standards have on business and to propose steps to counter his influence. Along the way, we can elevate the ethical standards of business generally, which seems to me a worthy, and profitable, antidote to the Trump model.

Four Actions to Follow

Reflecting on my own business principles and experience, discussing the subject with others equally appalled at Trump's actions, and absorbing the experiences and opinions of academics and business leaders generally, have all allowed me to condense my thoughts into four primary areas of action. They represent both general and specific steps that can be taken by business leaders at every level, in every industry and in every geographical region of the country. As you absorb them, I hope you realize their impact and influence. More than that, I hope you agree that standing by and permitting Trump to justify his rejection of ethics—personal and business—while serving in the leadership position he managed to achieve in 2016 is intolerable.

ACTION 1: DON'T PREACH IT—PRACTICE IT

Doing business in a principled way involves consistency, honesty, morality and trustworthiness, even in the face of adversity. It dispenses with pretense and advocates taking responsibility for your words and actions, refusing to cast blame on predecessors and subordinates.

The key is not only to identify values important to you and your organization, but to live them—actively ingrain them into the culture and the daily business practices of every employee. It starts at the top. Behind every ethical business is values-based leadership.

ACTION 2: BE BRAVE

Okay, it's lonely at the top. So what? Isn't that where you wanted to be? Standing up in defense of your own values and scruples may be difficult in some situations. But if your values are strong enough and run deeply enough within you, what is your choice? Denying these values is like denying your own identity. Acting in a manner that is consistent with your ethics will both define you personally and strengthen your organization in the long run. Trust, consistency and reputation are all built on values-based leadership and principled business practices, and their true worth becomes apparent when the going gets tough.

I have yet to see evidence of Donald Trump's bravery in either business or politics. He has threatened, he has bullied and, where he clearly was at odds with accepted behavior, he has pleaded ignorance. The best leaders, in both business and politics, draw on their moral courage to take the lead when unpopular but necessary action is called for. If you don't have that level of courage, I would question your qualifications for the job.

ACTION 3: KEEP YOUR PERSPECTIVE

Yes, as a leader you may need to work within an environment of often conflicting systems, values and personalities. No, this doesn't mean that you must join others in a race to the bottom where ethics are concerned. There may be no more childish phrase than "Everyone else was doing it!"

Your values belong to both you and your business. You cannot give up or dilute one set without weakening the other. Among the most important functions of leaders is to set, maintain and, if possible, elevate the status—moral, financial and reputational—of the entity they are managing. Lose that perspective, and you risk losing everything.

ACTION 4: DEVELOP SOCIAL INTELLIGENCE

Ethical behavior, in my opinion, goes beyond keeping rules in your mind. The rules are important to follow, but simple compliance will take you only so far. Following and acting on your principles rather than just sticking to the rules or the letter of the law is natural, intuitive and far more effective for your business.

When you are aware not only of moral standards to follow but of the motives and feelings of others and how they are affected by your actions, then ethics become as natural as breathing. This social intelligence, of course, presupposes a basic interest in being a decent person. If you choose to be a bully and assume that every encounter, either business or personal, is a zero-sum event, you shouldn't be reading this book.

Social intelligence becomes the means of building alliances with partners, understanding the motivations of customers, negotiating in good faith, and acting in a positive yet flexible manner toward others in your organization. I'm not sure if, like perfect pitch in music, you are born with the ability or you develop it as part of your maturity as an individual. I only know that the most effective leaders in business and politics all possess and apply it successfully. Those with an engaging manner do so to enormous success—think of Ronald Reagan and Bill Clinton. Far apart in their respective political positions, they were similar in their ability to grasp the attitudes and feelings of people and address them successfully.

Was this just natural charm on their part, or practiced craft? It doesn't matter. Not all of us are natural schmoozers, able to win over every person we meet with a warm smile and a perfect comment. But those of us who care about others we encounter, deal with them ethically and build their trust in us don't need the extreme likeability of a Reagan or a Clinton. You don't have to be buddies with staff, employees and business partners; you should, however, respect them and, in turn, be respected for the person you are. Your effectiveness as a leader will be measured by the way you treat others. You need only the intent to act ethically and the mind-set to see others as individuals with concerns similar to your own.

And here's another Decency Dividend: Treating everyone in your organization with respect by applying your social intelligence across the board prevents a wide range of potential concerns and conflicts. Your actions and attitude reduce or eliminate issues of sexual harassment, theft of materials and supplies, expense report padding and much more.[55] Take your social intelligence far enough with consistency and you may be able to reduce or eliminate many of your HR department's responsibilities entirely.

ETHICS, VALUES, TRUST, confidence, morals, integrity, principles—we all know these terms and their meaning. We also know that they represent the best sides of us as human beings, as individuals sharing the same planet for a disturbingly few decades of life. Some people, unfortunately, believe that these qualities may conflict with the primary goal of free enterprise—the ability to generate a reasonable profit from our energies, our ideas and our time. They are convinced that breaking their promises, ignoring truth and reality, and refusing to honor their commitments all pave the way to wealth and success.

They are wrong. In the end, people who conduct business without principles destroy themselves, and do terrible damage to their colleagues, their organizations and to those of us who emphasize truth and respect in our business dealings. They behave like bullies, and whatever sense of achievement and personal esteem they may cling to is a mirage, a product of their own unfettered ambition, a fraud.

Gandhi knew a thing or two about bullies and about the best way to conduct our lives not just as businesspeople but also as individuals who value self-respect and a sense of community. He deserves (almost) the last word on the topic:

> There are seven things that will destroy us: Wealth without work; Pleasure without conscience; Knowledge without character; Religion without sacrifice; Politics without principle; Science without humanity; Business without ethics.[56]

A Furious Final Word

FOR SEVERAL YEARS, I have wanted to write a book on my personal and business life, sharing the lessons I learned. I'm told it's not an unusual ambition, especially for those who rose through challenging times to achieve a goal that might have appeared unattainable at the beginning.

All of my attempts to draft the story lacked a key element and appeared unfocused. At one point I remembered a quote attributed to Beethoven, who said that playing a wrong note was insignificant but playing without passion was inexcusable. Despite hitting the right notes with my story, something appeared to be missing and I realized it was passion. So I put off the idea for a while. I told myself that I wasn't the only person to travel from a challenging childhood situation to a level of success and prosperity. Some, I'm sure, began in even worse circumstances and rose to greater wealth and power than me, yet they chose not to share the story of their journey with others. I understand their point of view and sympathize with it. For a while I chose to forget about writing a book and instead concentrated my time, effort and money on other things in life.

Then, Donald Trump was declared President of the United States of America. (It took a good deal of effort for me to write those words.)

When I recovered from the shock of November 8, 2016, I experienced many of the emotions that millions of other Americans were feeling. The election victory was wrong, unfair and frightening. But it was also motivating to me. Trump's election gave me the fire in my belly that I had needed. It inspired me to invest the time and energy to write this book on the importance of business ethics and values-based leadership.

It is no exaggeration to say that my business experience both saved and defined me. I value beyond measure the experiences I had, the goals I achieved and the people I dealt with as a business owner—employees, associates, clients and vendors. Work brought my wife, Cayce, and me together, leading to a family life that I cannot imagine being more fulfilling and thrilling. My professional life placed me smack in the middle of all that makes my chosen country so great—the American dream of being able to rise above the terrible milieu of one's origins to fulfill all of one's abilities and ambitions, and doing it while demonstrating full respect for others. That ideal has all been besmirched, in my opinion, by the actions of a man who, as I write this, occupies the top leadership position in America and the world.

Donald Trump was free to practice almost any political game he chose. The one he selected—a path of dubious values, absent ethics, constant bragging and bullying, and disrespect for all who dare choose to disagree with him—has damaged this country immeasurably, including the once-valued concept of business as a positive force. He has wounded the faith of many Americans in our electoral system and shattered the comforting belief that America's leaders behave with concern and respect for all. My fear is that his assertions about being a shrewd and successful businessperson will be taken seriously and will influence a number of people to believe that he is the model for business success and for how business should be conducted.

He is not. Nor will he ever be.

Acknowledgements

WITHIN DAYS OF Donald Trump's election victory, John Lawrence Reynolds and I met to discuss this book. I had drawn on John's writing talents over many of my years in business and was familiar with his abilities, and he proved fully adept at assisting me in expressing my concerns and outrage. His work on this book confirms his reputation as a superb researcher and writer, and cemented our friendship even more deeply.

The support of my wife and family through the many months of preparation has been invaluable. This book stands as a tribute to their faith in my values and determination, and justifies all the love and gratitude I feel for them in return.

I am also grateful for the superb team at Figure 1 Publishing for their professionalism and belief in the validity of my views. I never knew so many dedicated professionals beyond the authors were required to produce a book. Thanks to Chris Labonté, Jennifer Smith, Lara Smith, Karen Milner, Lindsay Humphreys, Renate Preuss and Naomi MacDougall for your talents and efforts.

Endnotes

1 "President-Elect Donald J. Trump Announces Travis Kalanick of Uber, Elon Musk of SpaceX and Tesla, and Indra Nooyi of PepsiCo to Join President's Strategic and Policy Forum." Great Again News Release, December 14, 2016.

2 "Trump's Lawsuits Unprecedented for a Presidential Nominee." *USA TODAY*, June 2, 2016.

3 "Donald Trump Questioned on His Bankruptcies." *International Business Times*, April 12, 2011.

4 Sara Germano, "New Balance Faces Social Media Backlash After Welcoming Trump." *Wall Street Journal,* November 10, 2016.

5 Will Grice, "New Balance's Trainer Sales 'Crashed in the U.S.' After They Backed Trump." *Metro News UK*, November 18, 2016.

6 Maggie McGrath, "Plank's Trump Praise Leads to Downgrades for Under Armour Stock." *Forbes,* February 15, 2017.

7 Fareed Zakaria, "The Unbearable Stench of Trump's B.S." *Washington Post*, August 4, 2016.

8 As quoted by Danielle Kutzleben in her review "Trump's New Book Doesn't Say Much, But Neither Do Lots of Political Books." Npr.org, November 5, 2015.

9 Gallup: Honesty/Ethics in Professions. December 14, 2016.

10 *Beyond Distrust: How Americans View Their Government*. Pew Research Center, November 23, 2015.

11 Ethisphere 2017 report on the world's most ethical companies. worldsmostethicalcompanies. ethisphere.com, accessed on August 5, 2017.

12 Peter Stone, "Donald Trump's Lawsuits Could Turn Off Conservatives Who Embrace Tort Reform." The Center for Public Integrity, May 5, 2011.

13 Abha Bhattarai and Catherine Ho, "Four Years Into Dodd-Frank, Local Banks Say This Is the Year They'll Feel the Most Impact." *Washington Post,* February 7, 2014.

14 Marshall Lux and Robert Greene, "The State and Fate of Community Banking." Mossavar-Rahmani Center for Business and Government/M-RCBG Associate Working Paper No. 37, Harvard Business School (2015).
15 David Bartstow and Akejandra Xanic von Bertrab, "The Bribery Aisle: How Wal-Mart Got Its Way in Mexico." *New York Times*, December 17, 2012.
16 Teddy Wayne, "The Culture of Nastiness." *New York Times*, February 18, 2017.
17 "Hannity." Fox News, June 17, 2015.
18 Milton Friedman, *Capitalism and Freedom*. (University of Chicago Press: 1962), p. 187.
19 John Paul Rollert, "How Sociopathic Capitalism Came to Rule the World." *The Atlantic*, November 2, 2016.
20 Ibid.
21 Advertising Age, *AdAge Encyclopedia of Advertising*. September 15, 2003.
22 Novartis 2016 Annual Report.
23 Jerry Knight, "Tylenol's Maker Shows How to Respond to Crisis." *Washington Post*, October 11, 1982.
24 Rogers Commission, "Report of the Presidential Commission on the Space Shuttle Challenger Accident." *Chapter V: The Contributing Cause of the Accident*, June 6, 1986.
25 Howard Berkes, "30 Years After Explosion, Challenger Engineer Still Blames Himself." NPR, *All Things Considered*, January 28, 2016.
26 "Top 10 Product Recalls: One Bad Bump." *Time Magazine*, July 02, 2009.
27 Laurie Burkitt, "Companies' Good Deeds Resonate with Consumers." *Forbes*, May 27, 2010.
28 Russell Hotten, "Volkswagen: The Scandal Explained." BBC News, December 10, 2015, plus various other sources.
29 Chris Paukert, "Volkswagen Emissions Scandal Could Cost $86 Billion, Report Says." CNET Road/Show, October 5, 2015.
30 Food Access Research and Education (FARE) at foodallergy.org, *Facts and Statistics*, accessed on February 8, 2017.
31 Roland E. Kidwell Jr. and Christopher L. Martin (eds.), *Managing Organization Deviance*. (Sage Publications, Inc.: 2005). Online publication date: May 31, 2012.
32 Ibid.
33 Aristotle, *Rhetoric*, BI, xii [Freese, trans.].
34 William N. White, "HBS Students Take Ethics Code." *Harvard Crimson*, June 2, 2009.
35 Archie B. Carroll, "The Pyramid of Corporate Social Responsibility: Toward the Moral Management of Organizational Stakeholders." *Business Horizons* (Volume 34, Issue 4 – July-August 1991), pp. 39–48. Used by permission.
36 Russell Freedman, with photographs by Lewis Hine, *Kids at Work: Lewis Hine and the Crusade Against Child Labor*. (Clarion Books: New York, 1994), pp. 54–57.
37 Scott Stump, "Donald Trump: My Dad Gave Me 'A Small Loan' of $1 Million To Get Started." CNBC, October 26, 2015.
38 Mason Levinson and Eben Novy-Williams, "Armstrong's Cheating Won Record Riches of More Than $218 Million." Bloomberg News, February 21, 2013.
39 William C. Rhoden, "For Soccer to Flourish in the U.S., Its Doors Must Open." *New York Times*, July 3, 2009.
40 *ProxyPulse*, Third Edition. Broadridge Investor Communication Solutions, Inc.
41 *Global Customer Service Barometer*. American Express, 2011.
42 Details of the collapse are drawn from "Joe Fresh Customers Vow Boycott After Bangladesh Factory Collapse" by Leslie Ciarula Taylor. *Toronto Star*, April 25, 2018.

43 Terri Williams, *Why Integrity Remains One of the Top Leadership Attributes.* The Economist Executive Education Navigator, accessed August 16, 2017.
44 Fred Kiel, *Return on Character: The Real Reason Leaders and Their Companies Win.* (Harvard Business Review Press: Boston 2015).
45 Herb Singer, *Grab The Wheel and Go!* (FriesenPress: 2016), p. 94.
46 *Race, Racism and the Law.* Racism.org, accessed on 21 August 2017.
47 Diversityinc.com, 2016: *Top 50 Companies For Diversity,* accessed on April 2017.
48 Catalyst Inc., *The Bottom Line: Connecting Corporate Performance and Gender Diversity,* accessed April 18, 2017.
49 D. Kirkpatrick, J.J. Phillips, and P.P. Phillips, "Getting Results From Diversity Training in Dollars and Cents." *HR Focus*, October 2003; 80, pp. 10–13.
50 Tripp Mickle, "Apple's Cash Stockpile Expected to Top a Staggering $250 Billion." *Wall Street Journal*, April 30, 2017.
51 Gathered from various sources. This summary is based on a feature posted by SparkPeople.com on November 19, 2016.
52 Stephen M. R. Covey, "The Business Case for Trust." *Chief Executive Magazine*, June 4, 2007.
53 Ibid.
54 Stephen M. R. Covey, *The Speed of Trust.* (Free Press/Simon & Schuster: 2006), p. 15.
55 Shira Levine, *The Importance of Keeping Your Integrity in Business.* American Express Open Forum, August 27, 2010.
56 The "Seven Social Sins" are derived from a list published by Ghandi in his weekly newspaper, *Young India,* on October 22, 1925.

Index

accountability, 17, 190
actuaries, 126–27
African-Americans, 179–80
agriculture, 19–20
Airbnb, 187
ambition, 128
American Youth Soccer Organization (AYSO), 140–41
Anderson, Maxwell F., 80
Apollo space program, 97
apparel companies, 159–61, 189–90
Apple, 166, 186–87
Aristotle, 52–53, 78
Armstrong, Lance, 131–32
Audi, 66*n*
automation, 5*n,* 185
automotive companies, 63, 64–65. *See also* Ford Motor Company; rental car companies; Volkswagen
Avis, 38
AYSO (American Youth Soccer Organization), 140–41
Bangladesh factory collapse, Dhaka, 160–61, 189–90
barriers, 127–28
basketball, 105
Bear Stearns, 76
Beethoven, Ludwig van, 203
Benefacts, 117
Berkshire Hathaway, 27*n,* 195
blindness, ethical, 57–58, 59–60
blueberries, 38
Boston Marathon, 132
bravery, 198–99. *See also* courage
bribery, 27, 85, 176
Broverman, Sherryl, 148–49, 150–51
Buffett, Warren, 27*n,* 30, 195
bullshit, 10–11
bureaucracies, 115–16
bureaucratic status, 114
business, future of
disruption examples, 186–87

need for ethics, 186, 188–90, 191
need for leadership changes, 188
predictions, 185, 187–88
business, right to exist, 56
business ethics
action despite better judgment, 54–56
action needed for implementation, 87, 198
approach to, xiii, xvii–xviii, 12–13, 18, 196–98
benefits from, 17, 22, 28, 37, 81, 84, 86–87
blindness to, 57–58, 59–60
bravery in, 198–99
vs. compliance, 31
connection to personal ethics, 79
costs of unethical practices, 6–7, 16–17, 18–19, 201
deserving beneficiaries, 158, 162
Enron's impact, 73–75
excuses for violations, 85–86
measurements of, 17–18
perspective needed for, 199
public perception of, 15–16
for regulatory decrease, 23–26
ripple effect of, 160
social intelligence for, 199–200
social media reflection of, 26–28
Trump's potential impact on, xi–xiii, xv–xvi, 8–10, 13, 16, 22–23, 131, 193, 197
unpopular vs. unethical decisions, 19–22
See also codes of ethics; ethics; leadership

car companies, 63, 64–65. *See also* Ford Motor Company; rental car companies; Volkswagen
Carnegie, Andrew, 30
cars, self-driving, 188
Caterpillar, 65
Challenger space shuttle, 54–56
cheating, 131–33
child labor, 81, 84, 84*n*
Chrysler, 65
Clinton, Bill, 200
Clinton, Hillary, 5
clothing companies, 159–61, 189–90
codes of ethics
to attract and keep employees, 173
to avoid negative publicity or litigation, 174–75
benefits of, 84–85, 169, 178
conciseness, 175
for difficult issues, 176–77
to encourage customer loyalty, 171–73
industry specificity, 175
input from stakeholders, 176
legal assistance in writing, 177
perspective in, 176
for positive workplace environment, 174
purpose of, 170–71
responsibility for, 177–78
See also business ethics
cold calls, 110–11
collaboration, 196
communities
business as, 18, 51–52
as context for business, 36–37, 56–57, 60–61
mutual benefit ideal, 34–35, 40–41, 161–62
Community Partnership Day, 40–41
compensation, executive, 86
competition, 20
computer industry, 186–87
confidentiality, 42
Conscious Capitalism (Mackey), 166
consequences, unintended, 24–25
consistency, 41

consumers and customers
desire to engage with businesses, 28
ethical demands and influence, 160–61, 191
ethical treatment of, 159
loyalty inspired by corporate ethical behavior, 171–73, 196
conventional individuals, 77
Cook, Tim, 166
Copeland, Misty, 7
Cordant Technologies, *see* Morton Thiokol
corporate citizenship (corporate social responsibility), 81, 82–83, 86–87
courage, 52, 128, 198–99
culture, corporate (workplace environment), 165–66, 174, 181. *See also* diversity; employees
Cummins, 65
Curry, Stephen, 7
customers, *see* consumers and customers

Daraprim, 67
Detroit Diesel, 65
Dhaka, Bangladesh factory collapse, 160–61, 189–90
Dickens, Charles, *A Tale of Two Cities,* 92
Dimon, Jamie, 9*n*
discrimination, 179–80
diversity
benefits and importance, 179, 180–81, 182–83
leadership role in encouraging, 181–82
research on benefits from, 183–84
DiversityInc., 183
Dodd-Frank Wall Street Reform and Consumer Protection Act, 25–26, 26*n*

education
author's experiences, 103–4, 106
economic impacts of, 84
Eichmann, Adolf, 48
Eisenhower, Dwight, 17
employee benefits packages, 115, 117–18
employees, 113–14, 158, 173, 176. *See also* culture, corporate
Enron
introduction, 71
attitude held by, 75–76
impact on business world, 73–75, 76–77
overview of fraud, 72–73
role of leaders in fraud, 76
similar examples to, 75, 76
entrepreneurs, 93
EpiPen, 68, 69
epiphanies, 96
ethics
author's interest in, 133–34
common approaches to, 77–78
definition, 31
vs. law, 171
personal, 79
understanding origins of, 92, 98
See also business ethics; codes of ethics; leadership
experience, learning from, 7*n*
Explorer (Ford SUV), 43–45

failure, business, 32
fairness, 39–40
Falconbridge Nickel Mines Limited, 100, 101, 102, 115
farm workers, migrant, 19–20
film industry, 186

financial regulatory system, 25–26
Firestone, 43–45
football, American, 12–13, 105
Forbes, Malcolm, 181
Ford Motor Company, 27–28, 28*n*, 43–45, 59–60, 65
Friedman, Milton, 34–35
future, *see* business, future of

Gandhi, 201
Gates, Bill, 30, 60
Gecko, Gordon, 30
Germany, 19*n*, 66
gig economy, 191
GM (General Motors), 65
Golden Mean, 52
Goldman Sachs, 76
Graham, Katherine, 30
Great Recession (2007–08), 9*n*, 25, 74, 76
growth, corporate, 39, 120, 196

Harvard Business School, 80–81
hats, 32–33
HealthSouth Corporation, 58–59
Hippocratic oath, 170, 170*n*
hockey, 105
honesty, 18, 37–39, 191

Iger, Robert, xiv
innovation, 196
insurance, life, 110–11
integrity
  corporate impacts of, 12, 165–67
  in leaders vs. rulers, 164–65
integrity, components of
  consideration of other's best interests, 40–41
  consistency, 41
  fairness, 39–40
  honesty, 37–39
  openness, 42–45
  trust, 45–46
Ironman Triathlon, 128–31, 133–34

Jobs, Steve, 186–87
Johnson & Higgens (J&H), 125–26, 127, 134–35
Johnson & Johnson, 42–43
judgment, acting against, 54–56

Kennedy, John F., 33
Kenya WISER program, 148–50, 150–51
Kiel, Fred, 166–67
Kodak, 186, 186*n*
Kroc, Ray, 30

LAFC (Los Angeles Football Club), 142
Latinos, 180
laws, 23–24, 171. *See also* regulations
Lay, Kenneth, 74
layoffs, 19, 40
leadership
  benefits from ethical, 165–66
  executive compensation, 86
  expectation of ethical conduct from, 8
  inability to resist authority by, 48, 50–51, 53, 54
  influence held by, 9, 29–30, 32–34
  influence on business ethics, xvi–xvii, 31–32, 74, 76, 77
  predictions on future role, 188
  role in encouraging diversity, 181–82
  vs. rulers, 164–65
  See also business ethics
legal profession, 187
Lehman Brothers, xvii, 76
life insurance, 110–11
listeriosis, 45

litigation, 174, 182, 194
location, retail, 21
Los Angeles, 96–97, 125–26
Los Angeles Football Club (LAFC), 142
loyalty, xv, 196
lying, 10–11

Mackey, John, 166
Mack Trucks, 65
Madoff, Bernie, xvii, 30
Malone, Cayce, 126, 148, 204
managers, 93
manufacturing offshore, 5, 5*n*, 19
Manufacturing Councils, xiv
Manulife, 106–7, 109–10, 111–12, 112–14, 115–16
Maple Leaf Foods, 45
Marcus Aurelius, 87, 162
marketing, 191
markets, 57
Marriott International, 28
McDonald's, 21
McLuhan, Marshall, 7*n*
medical profession, 187–88
Mercer, 117–18, 118–19, 121, 125
"middle of the road" approach, 52
migrant farm workers, 19–20
The Milgram Experiment, 48–50, 53
mission statements, 169–70
modeling theory, 77
Monterey Bay Aquarium, 170
Morton Thiokol, 55, 55*n*
Moss, Julie, 129, 130*n*, 133–34
mugging experience, 138–39
Muhuru Bay, Lake Victoria, WISER program, 148–50, 150–51
Musk, Elon, xiv
Muslims, 180, 181
Mylan, 68

NASA, 54–56, 97
Navistar, 65
nepotism, 177
New Balance Athletics, 3–5, 5–6, 8
Newman, Paul, 60
Nextel Communications, 184
Nike, 4
Nixon, Richard, 8
Novartis, 40–41

offshore sourcing, 5, 5*n*, 19
openness (transparency), 18, 42–45, 190
opportunity blindness, 58

parallel deviance, 74
Patterson, Merv, 112
PBS, 170
personal ethics, 79
personalities, dominant, 29
perspective, 176, 199
Peter Principle, 115
Pfizer, 68
pharmaceutical companies, 57, 67, 68–69
philanthropy, 60, 83, 151
Pinto (Ford car), 60
Plank, Kevin, 7
preconventional individuals, 77
principled individuals, 77
priorities, shift in, 95–96
profitability
  dividends from building trust, 194, 195–96
  excessive focus on as barrier to ethical behavior, 59–60, 64–66, 172
  executive compensation and, 86
  social considerations, 36–37, 68–70
Project GOAL, 147

promotion (marketing), 191
psychology, 47–48
publicity, negative, 7, 66, 85, 161, 174–75

Reagan, Ronald, 56, 200
reason, 52–53
regulations, 23–26, 174, 194
relationships, romantic, 176–77
Renault, 65
rental car companies, 38, 172–73
reputation, 7, 80, 134, 137–38, 189, 191
responsibility, 18
Responsibility Pyramid, 82–83
restrictions, 127–28
Return on Character (Kiel), 166–67
revelations, 96
robots, *see* automation
Rollert, John Paul, 36
Ruiz, Rosie, 132

sales, 111, 115–17, 120
Sanders, Bernie, 5
San Francisco, 123–24
Sarbanes-Oxley Act, 73, 194
Schwarzman, Stephen, xiv
Scrushy, Richard M., 59
Sears, 58
shareholders, 156–58, 162
Sheppard, Donald Lee (author)
  introduction, xvii, 91–92
  interest in ethics, 133–34
  motivation to write book, 203–4
  political leanings, 51
  priorities shift, 95–96
  relationship to U.S., 12
Sheppard, Donald Lee, career
  at Benefacts, 117
  costs from, 120–21
  early business lessons, 112, 113–14, 114–15, 119–20
  entrepreneurial focus, 94
  first job with Manulife, 106–7
  goals, 124–25
  integrity focus, 12
  at Johnson & Higgens (J&H), 125, 127, 134–35
  at Manulife, 109–10, 111–12, 112–14, 115–16
  at Mercer, 117–18, 118–19, 121, 125
  sales experience, 116–17
  at Sheppard Associates, 92–93, 94–95, 135–36, 137–38
Sheppard, Donald Lee, childhood
  childhood lessons, 98
  family background, 99
  father, 99–100
  school experiences, 103–4, 106
  sports involvement, 105–6
  teenage reputation, 104–5
  unions and strike experiences, 101–2, 102–3
Sheppard, Donald Lee, community engagement
  cross-America cycling trip, 146–48
  interest in, 96–97, 139
  in Kenya, 150–51
  soccer involvement, 139–43
Sheppard, Donald Lee, personal life
  Ironman Triathlon experience, 129–31
  marriage to Cayce, 126
  marriage to Sylvia, 120, 123
  move to Los Angeles, 125–26
  move to San Francisco, 121, 123–24
  mugging experience, 138–39
  sixty-fifth birthday reflections, 145–46

Shkreli, Martin, 67, 67*n*
Skilling, Jeffrey, 73
Smith, Adam, 35
soccer
introduction, 139–40
American Youth Soccer Organization (AYSO), 140–41
author's involvement, 140–41, 142–43
club soccer, 141–42
social intelligence, 199–200
social media, 22, 26–28, 30–31, 189, 190, 191
Southwest Airlines, 28
space program, 54–56, 97
SPCA, 170
special-purpose entities (SPES), 72
sports, 105–6, 131–33
Starbucks, 20–22, 28, 34
status, bureaucratic, 114
strikes, 101–2
Sudbury (ON), 99, 99*n*
Sudbury Basin, 97–98, 98*n*
suppliers (vendors), 159–61

A Tale of Two Cities (Dickens), 92
TBR (To Be Reversed) invoices, 134–35
Templeton, John, 58*n*
Toronto, 124
Toyota, 65
Trans-Pacific Partnership (TPP), 4–5, 5*n*
transparency (openness), 18, 42–45, 190
Trek Travel, 146
Trump, Donald
background, 91
disassociation of businesses from, 163–64
disrespect by, 179
election as president, xvi
impact on U.S. image, xv, 204
inability to govern, xiv–xv
influence held by, 30–31, 33, 34, 53–54
lack of trust in, 46
Manufacturing Councils, xiv
need to resist, 51, 197–98
potential impact on business ethics, xi–xiii, xv–xvi, 8–10, 13, 16, 22–23, 131, 193, 197
public dislike of, xvi, 8
as ruler vs. leader, 164, 165
support for, 9, 197
unethical dealings, 32
use of bullshit, 10–11
worldview of, 35, 36, 40
Trump creep, 30–31
Trump Steaks, 32*n*
Trump University, 32
trust
associated virtues, 165
implications of lost trust, 35–36, 38, 86
importance of, 45–46, 194
profitability from, 194, 195–96
in workplace environment, 174
Turing Pharmaceuticals, 67
Tylenol, 42–43, 43*n*

Uber, 187
Under Armour, 7–8
unintended consequences, 24–25
unions, 101–2, 102–3
United Airlines, 155–56, 156*n*, 171–72, 175
United States of America
author's relationship with, 12
civil disagreement, xvi, 8
differences from business, xiii–xiv
loyalty of federal officials, xv
president's influence, 30

public perception of government ethics, 15–16

values, *see* business ethics; codes of ethics; ethics; leadership
vendors (suppliers), 159–61
Volkswagen, 63–64, 65–66, 175
Volvo, 65
vows, 81

Walmart, 27, 27*n,* 195
Warren, Elizabeth, 26*n*
Washington, Booker T., 30
Welch, Jack, xiv
Whole Foods, 28, 166
WikiLeaks, 189
women, 112, 180, 190
Women's Institute for Secondary Education and Research (WISER), 147, 148–50, 150–51
workplace environment (corporate culture), 165–66, 174, 181. *See also* diversity; employees
Wyatt, Watson, 195

Young Life Capernaum, 147